IN
MONTAIGNE'S
TOWER

IN
MONTAIGNE'S
TOWER

Essays by
Hilary Masters

University of Missouri Press

COLUMBIA AND LONDON

Library of Congress Cataloging-in-Publication Data

Masters, Hilary.
     In Montaigne's tower / Hilary Masters.
          p.   cm.
     ISBN 0-8262-1266-2 (alk. paper)
          I. Title.
     PS3563.A82 I52 2000
     814'.54—dc21   99-047635

⊗™ This paper meets the requirements of the
American National Standard for Permanence of Paper
for Printed Library Materials, Z39.48, 1984.

Text design: Elizabeth K. Young
Cover design: Susan Ferber
Typesetter: BookComp, Inc.
Printer and binder: Thomson-Shore, Inc.
Typeface: Perpetua

**FOR
KATHLEEN**

Books by Hilary Masters

Novels

The Harlem Valley Trio
Clemmons
Cooper
Strickland

Home Is the Exile
Manuscript for Murder
Palace of Strangers
An American Marriage
The Common Pasture

Short Fiction

Success
Hammertown Tales

Memoir

Last Stands: Notes from Memory

Essays

In Montaigne's Tower

Contents

IN
MONTAIGNE'S
TOWER

Going to Cuba

A sketch by Chekhov recounts the incident of two rural constables escorting an old vagrant to the local workhouse. The day is hot and their journey has been long and dusty. They decide to rest a little by the side of the road. The old man has refused to tell them his name or where he is from, but as he relaxes on the ground, he begins to spin a fancy of his homeland—a place of wondrous plenty. Clear, cool streams from which fish leap to catch themselves on lines. Berries and fruits fall ripe into outstretched hands. Milk and honey and always fair weather. His description enthralls the other two; they are carried away by his fantasy. Then, one of them snaps out of it, and they get back on the road. But, for a moment, both prisoner and police have been set free.

Our imaginations, often falsely confirmed by memory, can cross many borders, but these escapes are doomed and freedom always lies just beyond. For example, if I were to go out my door here on Monterey Street in Pittsburgh, take a right at the YMCA on the corner, then continue in a southeasterly direction across the point where the Allegheny and the Monangahela Rivers agree to become the Ohio, and then, if I were still to continue this same range athwart the southern states, my next landfall would be Cuba. Just beyond Cuba lies the Isle of Pines.

"Where is the Isle of Pines?" It is August of 1951, and the basement dive of Louis's on Sheridan Square is a frosty enclave within the steamed province of Greenwich Village. Rosemary Clooney is singing "C'mon to My House," and the woman who has just sat down at my table has jumped up to dance to the quasi-Arabic melody, swaying in her summer dress to the blast of the jukebox. No one takes any notice of her; she moves within a cell of her own, a figurine turning within a bell jar.

Someone is always playing the song, always feeding the jukebox so that Clooney sings without let-up until closing time, which it is close to right now. Three A.M. Just before, while Clooney takes a break, this blonde walks over from the bar and sits down at my table. She doesn't seem to be with anyone, and she carries a worn, leather portfolio under one arm. Out of this folder, she has taken a newspaper clipping and hands it to me. She is

1

very pale with stringy hair and eyes of beer-bottle green that seem to slide off into the whites around the pupils.

"C'mon to my house, c'mon to my house . . . c'mon," Clooney starts up again. "I give you ca-nn-dy."

This woman has just asked me to go to Cuba with her, to the Isle of Pines, then jumps up to dance by herself, not waiting for my answer nor hearing my question. Her bare feet pivot and shuffle on the sawdusted floor of the bar and she gives herself to the music in a way that seems to be a demonstration of something. I think of the women in Robinson Jeffers poetry. Wild. Primitive. Probably, dangerous.

So when she sits down, I have to ask her again. She is a little breathless and tastes a droplet of moisture above her lips before she answers.

"It's an island off the south coast of Cuba," she tells me. "I own a hundred acres on the beach. They've discovered oil on my property. What do you think?" She's motioned to the newspaper clipping in my hand. "Will he die?"

The picture that goes with the article shows the mangled wreckage of a Jaguar convertible smashed against a large tree. In Cleveland or Columbus. The horrific hybrid has produced a senseless being who, the account says, lies in a coma, near death in a hospital. His injuries are severe and numerous. "Do you think he'll die?" she asks once more.

"Doesn't look good," I say. Her expression is distant, a gaze for a moor or some desolate tundra, and I see not a shadow of concern or anxiety. Only a cool calculation. "Do you know him?"

"He's my husband," she says. "As soon as the son of a bitch dies, I'm going to Cuba. Why don't you come with me? The Isle of Pines."

Going to Cuba. In the smoky, mechanical frigid zone of Louis's, the tropical island rises in my imagination like a great ship, safely anchored in an artery waiting for the flood tide. The smell of disinfectant from the men's room becomes the aroma of conifers. I can see the surf curling around the beach like a cuff of lace.

This summer of 1951, I have been attending lectures in Anglo-Saxon and Old English at Columbia to make up for courses I slept through during the previous year at my home university. My GI bill is about to run out, but I am not all that interested in finishing my degree; not at my university which has become a preppy, hostile perimeter around my dreams of becoming a writer. Some of my contemporaries were already living in the Village and chatting up the resident literati at places like Chumley's or The White Horse. I wasn't even living in the Village, and my time in New York was given to making up failed courses. My contemporaries have already jumped into the currents of their careers as copyboys at the *Times* or UPI or into lower-echelon jobs in publishing, freelancing reviews in magazines.

I don't want a career; I want experience. I want to write and didn't Hemingway say to become a writer, experience had to be gained. And where was he getting his experience? Cuba.

Moreover, Delmore Schwartz and Dwight McDonald are not my mentors as they are for others. My current master is the poet Maxwell Bodenheim whose watery-eyed perception of my apprenticeship, as I would sit across from him at the San Remo, tested no more of my potential than the next cheap Chianti. What would Max think of this offer, I ask myself in Louis's? Would he pick up and go to the Isle of Pines with this strange woman?

Where is the Isle of Pines?

Off the coast of Cuba, Max. Should I go there to write?

Hell, yes, go there. These Chicago winters are going to kill me one day.

Of course we are in New York so Bodenheim is wrong on both counts, but I still give serious consideration to this willowy blonde's offer. It is nearly three A.M. at Louis's in Greenwich Village on Sheridan Square. Dancing in her bare feet, self-absorbed and strangely calm, I decide to call her Tamar. Red, the bartender whose hair is actually on the silvery side, begins to ease people over their final beers.

"Well, he's still alive," Tamar reports. She's just returned from the pay phone at the back, after taking all the change I had. A small enough investment, I have reasoned.

"You called the hospital?" Was it Akron or Toledo?

"He's still in a coma. Pelvis smashed. What's the thorax?"

"Chest." Red has caught my eye and looks meaningfully at the stairs that lead up to the street.

"That too," she says. The Jaguar had been traveling at a terrific rate of speed and the driver had been very drunk.

The summer's anthem starts up once more and Clooney lah-de-dahs Saroyan's lyrics as if they were an epilogue for the evening. Cleverly, I make a deft transition. "C'mon to my house—c'mon," I croon to this pallid creature with eyes that seem to have no back to them. As we climb the steps into the humid heaviness of the August night, I am thinking that no troubadour could have done better with his Auvergne shepherdess.

This summer, I am driving a 1946 Ford Anglia that looks like a normal car from the side, but, on turning a corner, the vehicle nearly becomes a vertical line, like a car in cartoons. Also, the floorboards on the passenger side are sketchy and my passenger's skirt billows in the updraft like a spinnaker as she holds her cracked sandals in her lap. We put-put up 7th Avenue, still a two-way thoroughfare, and Tamar hugs her briefcase and seems to enjoy the ride.

Yet, I expect her to have me stop at any moment as we journey north, and I run a couple of lights so as not to give her the chance to change her mind. There's a cool madness about her that suggests her natural habitat lies below 14th Street, and I wonder if to transport her into the rarefied atmosphere of the Upper West Side might wring a mortal change in her. I glance at her face. Her features remain composed in their fixed serenity; no sudden wrinkling around the eyes, no catastrophic hollowing of the cheeks.

"Who is this Tamar you keep calling me?" she asks when we join Broadway at 34th.

Indeed, I have renamed her—a preliminary to possession that at least one of us recognizes—though my nomination has dubious authority because of my confusion of Jeffers's heroines. I've mixed up the murderous, hot-blooded Tamar with the barefoot loving shepherdess who gives up her life defending her lambs; a confusion I am to have with more than one woman.

As we go up Broadway, I give her a quick gloss of Jeffers's poetry, at least my study of it in my father's library a few years back where the falling line accounts of lust between brother and sister, woman with woman and even—I leave this out—woman with stallion often inspired a sexual frenzy in me not experienced since reading Zola and Maupassant.

"There's a phone booth," she says suddenly. We are passing through the intersection of 57th Street, Columbus Circle just ahead, and the doings at Point Sur have held no interest for her.

"You just called the hospital, just before we left Louis's," I say and keep my foot down on the gas pedal. The Anglia's four cylinders are generating a lot of heat and sweat is popping out on my brow, trickling down from my armpits. The little car has become a portable oven. But Tamar looks cool and comfortable, though I wonder how she will be in my small room on 104th Street. One window on the building's air shaft. One small sink in the corner and one chair. The stale sheets on the narrow bed, where only this afternoon, I listlessly studied the conjugation of *lufian,* a traditional paradigm of a weak verb and meaning "to love."

"Maybe he's had a sinking spell," Tamar reasons.

"I don't have any more silver," I say.

"We can get change," she says.

"Where? It's after three in the morning!"

"In a subway. They make change all night in the subway."

I press on. The Anglia is making all the sequential green lights on Central

Park West, all in one run. On our right, the park looks inviting, a more natural and attractive alternative to my close and sultry room, but I'm afraid her Jeffers persona might take over. I can imagine her running off, barefoot, into the urban woods around the Reservoir to emerge on the East Side and gone forever.

Even when I park across from my building, I still expect her to flee downtown, but she follows me almost meekly across the street and waits, shoes in hand, as I unlock the apartment's main door. As we rise in the elevator, I am thinking that I am about to *lufian* a woman who is almost a widow, that to lie between her thighs, I will replace a man who lies horribly mangled and near death because of a passion that had driven him into a sycamore tree. The elevator labors to altitude and my heart spins like a turbocharger. That Tamar travels light and has no place to sleep has not occurred to me.

But this summer of 1951, I am borrowing more than books from my father's library and the urgencies of mind and matter they inspire. His history has also become a study for me, a curiosa to browse. He has just died the year before, and this final abandonment has led me to trace his and my mother's path around New York, to follow the outline of their lives, lived without me, before it becomes grown over in memory. Like a child who puts on a parent's clothes to gain intimacy, I have been putting on the accoutrements of my parents' history so that I might come to know them better. It is, of course, a charade and like all "dress-up" games made silly by daylight.

Until I was fourteen, my maternal grandparents cared for me in Kansas City, Missouri. My mother left me with them when I was able to make the transfer from breast to bottle, at a year old, and returned to New York to be with my father. Their reasons for this arrangement I have put down in a family biography, *Last Stands: Notes from Memory,* but they still mystify me.

However, she would return for brief visits, sometimes to take me back to New York for a week or two with my father, then return me to my grandmother's house on Roberts Street. Her entrances into that small house were always noisy and exciting as if the Barnum and Bailey parade had turned off of Independence Avenue to come down our street. She spoke of restaurants they had eaten at, important writers and artists they had met, of the artists' studios visited in Greenwich Village. She was like the press agent for a calamitous, triumphant road show though I am to learn later that these outlandish advertisements of their life were mostly fabricated to convince her parents the marriage was okay, that all was well and to court the stern opinion of her father by this show of success.

To listen to her, my parents seemed to own Greenwich Village and much of the rest of Manhattan. In Kansas City, I became acquainted with the Jumble Shop on the corner of McDougal and 8th Street. I could visualize the lobbies of the Brevort and the Lafayette Hotels and the funny things that went on there. I heard about exotic places like Romany Marie's and a German restaurant that sounded Chinese—Luchows. In 1951, Greenwich Village has not changed so much from their day, but I know little more about their passage through it. I cannot afford to enter Charles French Restaurant, where my father was supposed to favor the crepes, nor can I find Romany Marie's. Edna Millay's little house, she has just died also, is just as my mother described it and so is the Greenwich Mews where Mae Mott Smith had her studio. The inner courtyard of Patchin Place looks the same through the iron grill gate, though I'm not sure of the unit where the Welsh novelist John Cowper Powys served them tea by a cozy fireplace.

"e.e. cummings lives there now," I tell Tamar. This is later in the week, and that afternoon we have just made reservations to fly to Havana. She is impatient to take flight—probably, impatient with my guided tour as well. She looks around 6th Avenue for a phone booth. So even as she calls Akron or Toledo, I am trying to put on parts of my parents' life, none of which fit me even if I could afford the garb.

The little sum I have managed to save from my GI allowance is supplemented by the four bucks earned every weekday in a delicatessen in the garment district. This goes mostly for beers at Louis's or an occasional symposium with Bodenheim at the San Remo. Every day, starting at eleven and after my classes at Columbia, I take orders over the phone for sandwiches and bagels, custards and jello puddings that are then delivered by a couple of black kids to nearby offices. These guys, like me, also get their lunch, and, at the end of our stint, the three of us are given brown-bag bonuses of bagels, containers of cream cheese, and potato salad. Sometimes a little lox or a piece of brisket. These provisions usually do me for supper.

But I envy the delivery boys for they get something extra. Their lunchtime missions take them into the frenetic environs where women's clothing is being designed and fabricated, where the silken confinements of women's bodies were being fitted and fastened in place at such a fever pitch that the very sandwiches delivered probably lay half-eaten at the end of the day.

"Where are you going?" Tamar's voice is muffled this first morning; her face is pressed into the one pillow on the bed. The shade drawn down to the windowsill flaps idly in a humid breeze to play a brilliant scarf of light upon her naked rump. "We're just getting to sleep."

I am painfully aware of this fact as I slowly pull on my clothes. "I have to go to work," I tell her. My body is sore, blood has been drawn. She is everything Robinson Jeffers had claimed she would be. I tell her about my job, that I'll be back in a few hours and she should get some sleep. Delicacy keeps me from mentioning that I had missed my eight o'clock class in Old English. The small gash just below my rib cage, Tamar's nails were long and crimson, had happened just as everyone else was discussing the position of the negative *ne* before the verb, a convention that was to disappear with Middle English. That had been part of the day's assignment.

Tamar has slipped into a deep sleep.

My responses to the telephone rings at the delicatessen are Pavlovian perfect. As I take down orders for cheese-and-ham sandwiches, I review the other hot work that has only recently employed me. Tamar enclosed our lust within narratives, her feathery voice recounting details of her married life, and this running account inspired reenactments of that history. More than once in the hours before dawn, she had risen from the swampy mire of my narrow bed to talk about her husband, the man whose death we waited on. She had shivered, the chill of her own cooling sweat upon her, as she told me the things he had done to her. Her jolly breasts trembled like the noses of lambs.

"He would take me downtown to the finest stores," she told me. "Take me and buy me wonderful clothes. Go with me into the fitting rooms as I tried everything on. Everything. And everything was expensive. Underwear of lace and silk. Nylon stockings. Slips. Then dresses, blouses. Everything. He'd buy all these things. Then, at home, he has me go into the bedroom and put everything on and then, he would come into the bedroom. He would rip all these new, beautiful clothes off of me. Tear them off. Everything. Sometimes he would use scissors and cut them off. Everything. Cut them to ribbons. If I were wearing a blouse, he would take both his hands and rip it apart so the buttons would pop off on the floor. Pop-pop-pop." She demonstrated the attack, pulling her fists away from her chest suddenly and her breasts looked even more naked in the dim light. She panted as if she had just crossed the finish line of a race.

"No kidding," I said. "Why did he do that?" The man's wastefulness appalled me.

She had no answer, none that she could articulate, for she frowned a little. Then the scrap of a smile curled her lips. "Sometimes, he would tie me to one of the bed posts. We had an antique fourposter with a lacy canopy above. And then." A sudden fatigue slurred her voice and pulled at her eyelids.

"And then?" My bed was little more than a studio couch.

" . . . unspeakable things," Tamar whispered in my ear and pulled me down with her into the stew of another feverish reverie.

As always, I have used the subway this morning, leaving the Anglia parked across from my apartment. Sometimes, I would leave the car there for days—this is 1951 after all. So, when I walk from the subway on Broadway and 103rd and round the corner of Central Park West, I find Tamar sitting on the front step of my building, holding her white sandals in one hand and shielding her eyes with the other to peer into the territory of Central Park across the way. She looks fragile and forlorn, bleached to a near transparency by the midday heat and resembles one of those prairie women in a Walker Evans photograph. Instantly, I know she had dressed and gone out of the building to phone Ohio and has not been able to get back in.

"He's developed pneumonia," she says as she rises to greet me. Her gaze looks hopefully at me for confirmation—this is a good sign?

"How about something to eat?" I hold up the bag of goodies from the deli.

We find some shade under a tree in the park, and I lay out the provisions on a flat piece of black shale, feeling very much the gatherer returned from the hunt. I have set down bagels, cream cheese, and pieces of pressed ham. My employers have also thrown in a couple of pretty ripe bananas. The day has become beastly hot. "We could use some *showres sote*," I say.

"Sure," Tamar nods and smiles. "But, maybe we can get a Coke or something later." She is an oracle who knows the answer and isn't telling.

She picks at the ham and makes ladylike decisions, taking one piece rather than another, while holding the bagel in a unique style. She's stuck her index finger through the hole and nibbles around the edges as if to acknowledge the bagel's design, if not suggest the original mode of its consumption, perhaps just discovered in Ohio.

Sucking off the ham residue from her fingers, she uses this hand to open the soft leather portfolio that seems to be her only baggage. I see handkerchiefs and cosmetics, some underclothing and folders of papers that have a valuable appearance. Perhaps, there's a will among them. Some have borders printed in pale blue and brown like bonds. She has pulled out a different kind of document. Its many folds are worn thin, completely through in some places, and she carefully lays it out on the rock, taking small bites around the bagel. She has unfolded a survey map.

"Here is my property. See here's the beach. The town of Nueva Gerons is just a few miles this way." She points off the map to where ants are busy in a crack in the rock. The printing is in Spanish. Lines cross and intersect. "The house is old, but we can live in it while we build a new one. Closer to the beach. You'll be able to hear the trade winds as you write. They will ruffle your hair and your papers."

"How do you come to own this place?"

"My mother left it to me. See here is her name at the bottom. *Pro-pie-tario.* And they have discovered oil on the property."

"Yes, you told me. You've been there, you've seen it?"

Her yellow hair flags down my question for its triviality. "Of course not. How could I?" I have no answer for that. "Pan American flies to Havana," she continues. "We must make reservations. From Havana, we take the train, only an hour or two, to the port of Batabano. Then we take a small boat, probably a ferry, across the gulf. To my island."

Only then, I admit to myself, I have been going along with this story of hers—the Isle of Pines and the rest of it—not just to get her into my bed, but to tease this fantasy I have of a writer's life. One should be comfortable while entertaining the Muse and, like most young writers, I thought the workplace was crucial to the work. Even, one and the same. Warm weather, sandy beaches, and all the mangoes you can eat—that's where the real work is to be done. Look at Hemingway! So, it is a scary moment for me when I realize that I believe her. Here in the tropical simmer of Central Park, this strange woman has laid out for me the deed to a fantasy. It's the genuine article. She does own part of a Caribbean island. She does want to take me there. This worn and ravaged angel landed next to me at Louis's and has offered me a dream, a shortcut to literary success.

Tamar has begun to fold up the map, her expression cheerful and eyes downcast. Her face is pink with the heat. She only uses one hand, demonstrating an expertise with the map's seams and double rucks, while she continues to take bites of bagel impaled on the other. She's nibbled it down to a small ring around her finger which, with a demure glance, she slips deep into her mouth to pull off the last morsel.

By chance, my grandfather had sent me one of the several pension checks he receives every month for his different services as a young man, subduing natives on the western frontier or parts of Central America. As we share the better banana of our picnic, I think it would be nice to buy Tamar some new shoes and then take her to dinner someplace. An outlet store near the subway on Broadway has stacks of name-brand shoes marked down to very low prices. She will step ashore on the Isle of Pines in decent footwear at least. I could buy her a new dress also, but she might get the wrong idea.

She wears the stiff leather sandals with a quiet delight to dinner that night at Schiavi's, an Italian place in the west 30s near the main post office on 8th

Avenue. "My mother used to bring me here when I was on vacations from school. Christmas time mostly." Tamar helps herself to more soup from the tureen and says nothing. "Same place, same meal but only a dollar in those days. The lady at the cash register with the dyed red hair is Mrs. Schiavi. She looks the same too."

I am to learn that these dinners, cheap as they were, always put my mother in hock for a little. She and my father had separated by then, and she had just been hired to teach composition and literature at the Bentley School on West 86th Street. Her salary was one thousand dollars a year. So, every time I arrived at the Greyhound Terminal on 34th Street, only a couple of blocks from where Tamar and I are sipping the minestrone, my mother would have already visited a pawn shop, putting up the silver pepper grinder and the paired salt dish to raise a few bucks to stake me to a little holiday. These had been wedding gifts and she always managed to buy them back, for they sit on my dining room table today.

With the third course of roast chicken, following a plate of ravioli, I am telling Tamar about significant moments in my parents' lives at Luchows or Harry Bleak's, further uptown. How, one time, they encountered the publisher Horace Liveright just after Dreiser had thrown a cup of hot coffee on him. That happened at the Brevort. Or it might have been the Lafayette. Tamar does not demand accuracy, nor even the account itself. Something in her face tells me she is listening to an inner narrative of her own, a firsthand memoir and much more authentic. Before the meal, she had called the hospital in Ohio. The pneumonia seems to have been checked, but there are signs of liver failure. Tamar picks up part of her chicken and solemnly tears into the crisp thigh with her pearly teeth.

Several nights later, we walk around the Village, and I try to find Romany Marie's, but we end up in a chop suey joint a block from Louis's. After the fortune cookies, with what seem to be fatuously modest forecasts, we get over to Louis's and Tamar heads for the telephone just as Zack walks in.

Zack graduated the year I entered the university and is a bit older than I and well on his way to becoming a successful hack. In fact, he is about to transfer his patronage from Louis's to the White Horse and the rest, to use one of his phrases, is history. But, at the moment, he is working for a skin magazine cutting out pictures of pin-up models, separating the breasts and buttocks and then pasting them up in various provocative layouts to illustrate the magazine's articles. I am happy to see Zack because he has spent some time in Cuba and supposedly had even got drunk with Hemingway a couple of times, though this turns out to be one of his better fictions.

"You look terrible," he says first off as he sits down. "What's the matter—have you been sick?"

"Not getting much sleep," I say. "You know, hitting the books." Then I tell him, all at once, about Tamar and about going to Cuba. "We made the reservations today," I tell him. And this is true. I phoned the airline from one booth in Grand Central Station while Tamar called the hospital from another.

"For Cuba?" Zack asks.

"Yeah. Pan American. To Havana." I can't help myself and start to giggle.

Zack has nodded approval of the chosen airline, but he's not too familiar with the Isle of Pines. "Not as many pine trees as you might think," he does say.

"And they've discovered oil on the place."

"I have heard that is true," he says and sips his beer. "And this woman owns something there, you say?"

His interest pleases me. Usually, my role in this acquaintanceship is that of a loyal audience for the presentations of his success, of his chummy times with noted authors—what, for example, Norman Mailer had said to him only last week. So, I'm flattered by the attention he has been giving my theory about the workplace—how one's work is surely enriched by the long view. How the perception of one's culture can be sharpened, if not deepened, by living in another society. His eyes attend me closely as I speculate on the effect that living on a tropical island might have on metaphor.

Zack has been sipping his beer as he reviews my different theories and then he says, "A dream empowered can be a dangerous thing." He takes another sip and ruminates this wisdom. I am wondering if he's read it somewhere, say chiseled on the facade of a bank. But then, he says, "Look at Hitler," and he leans back in his chair and hugs himself. "Not to mention the German people."

Then, Tamar is back and sits down in the chair between us. She looks down shyly as I make the introductions but she is obviously aware of Zack's intense study. Her ears and the edges of her nostrils have become rabbit pink and there is a tremulous quiver along the line of her narrow lips. Maybe her husband has died, I think. We're off to Cuba tomorrow if that's the case. She has been on the phone longer than usual, perhaps making arrangements for the disposal of the body. I'll have to get my shirts out of the Chinese laundry on Amsterdam Avenue. I am busting to find out, but can say nothing in front of Zack.

Someone has punched Clooney's numbers again and the familiar ditty rattles through the place. Tamar jumps and leaves us as suddenly as she has arrived, like a bird lighting and then taking off again. She moves in her peculiar ritual before the altar of the jukebox, barefoot again. The new sandals are primly lined up on the floor beneath the table.

"That's the one?" Zack asks, his eyes level with mine.

"Yeah," I reply, enjoying his look. He shifts around to regard Tamar. She is slowly twisting in place, arms over her head and self-absorbed. Zack has verified everything. "By the way," I say, "do you know where Romany Marie's is? You know your way around the Village. Do you know what street it's on?"

Zack turns back. "It's around here somewhere. That's one of those old-time places nobody goes to anymore. That's one of those places you talk about like you were part of those old days. Like you have a history around here. You know, you are kind of ridiculous, trying to impress people with these names you are always introducing into conversations. You don't know anything about the Village or what's going on."

He gets up and moves to the bar and instantly goes head to head with another guy and the two of them are like secret agents or long-lost brothers. I have always envied this easy camaraderie Zack enjoys with others, for his being recognized already as "an old hand," but tonight I am filled with a pity for him that I do not quite understand. I do understand the accompanying exultation I feel.

My mother is now ninety-four years of age and lives in a nursing home several hours' drive from Pittsburgh. From my doorway here on Monterey Street I take an easterly route to Altoona where I turn almost due north to the town of Bellefonte. Talleyrand, my mother says, named the town during some tour of the new United States, perhaps when he was selling the Louisiana Territory to Tom Jefferson.

The territory beyond Altoona is very beautiful, a landscape that rises in undulant levels into the Nittany Range of the Allegheny Mountains and these long drives have become like retreats for me, isolated though movable studies where I peruse my memory's archives. Mile after mile, I come upon unexpected views, a turn of perspective, as the scenery changes.

Memory is a room always hitched to our travels, and, as we get older, its dimensions grow smaller so that certain artifacts are tossed out. We dispose of those items that no longer suitably furnish the image of a past we wish to keep; and if any clocks are kept, they are not kept going. Sometimes, this economy, this autumn cleaning, if you will, makes room for totally new fittings, fanciful stuffs to refurbish a dark corner or redo an unsightly composition.

My mother is enjoying this kind of redecoration lately which often puts her childhood days on the Panama on the same level with events she reads of in the daily newspaper. The journalist Vincent Sheehan, her university classmate of seventy-five years ago, is a contemporary of the late Senator John Heinz. She describes with great detail the memorial plinths being raised to both men; Sheehan's sarcophagus will be placed atop his column. Also, when she has moved things around in her memory, making certain substitutions, she finds the results often settle debts for services rendered her, as well as slights; and that these rearrangements in her memory often make it unnecessary to acknowledge a debt or even to express gratitude. *Please* has always been difficult for her to say and *thank you*, nearly impossible.

Last week, she sits in her wheelchair and stares out through an immense wall of glass at the wintered plainness of the garden outside. We are on the ground floor of the nursing room, a large multipurpose room with a small library in one corner, television in another and, near us, a large plastic Christmas tree. Tiny lights blink on and off. The ornaments are like those children might make and hang. Across the way, white-suited attendants are enjoying their lunch break, eating sandwiches while following a soap opera on the television.

My mother seems mesmerized by her barren prospect, her own being suspended in a kind of wonder of the still life outside the window. She resembles a Celtic crone, still not believing the spell that has changed her from the young colleen she really is inside, that has just changed her from the boisterous, fun-loving woman, I can remember, busting into our house in Kansas City to tell about the sprees she and my father had been having in New York. The women across the way have not moved, caught up in their TV melodrama.

We have gone through the topics of our usual discourse; the poor quality of the food served here, the insensitive handling by some of the attendants, the condition of her bowels. From A to Z, so to speak. Sometimes, I will throw a line into the subsequent silence to pull out a familiar story, practiced so many times that the parts of it slip into the narrative with a worn carelessness. I feel as if I am attending one of those ingenious robots Casanova described that amazed eighteenth-century Venetians with their chess play until it was disclosed that within each was a clever midget.

Just to try something different last week, I ask, "Where was Romany Marie's?"

She blinks. The trance has been broken. Her large eyes turn upon me as her withered lips taste the air. "Why on Washington Square, of course. Washington Square South."

"No, it moved from there."

"It did? When did it move?"

"A long time back. A Gypsy place, wasn't it?"

"Yes, Italian Gypsy," she says and leans toward me. "When your father and I went there, it was still Prohibition. Marie made her own wine and would serve it to us in coffee cups, with saucers, so the police wouldn't find out." Her laughter is old and soundless but a youthful gleam has shot through her eyes, a triumphant glee.

"But you don't remember where the restaurant moved?"

"No. Why do you want to know?" Her mouth chews on the question.

I have no answer; in fact, I am trying to find that answer as I write right now; so, I toss another line into her memory. "What about Hitler?"

Her eyes become even younger, luminous. "Well, she and her mother couldn't get out of France because—you know. The Germans were going to put them in one of those camps. I knew if I could just distract the man they called Hitler, then they could sneak by." She leans forward and puts one arm behind herself, motions the hand.

"So, you went up to Hitler and distracted him?"

"What?"

"You distracted him."

"I placed my little, soft child's fingers on his hands and went like this with my fingertips. His hands were dry and papery to the feel. And she and her mother were able to walk behind me, past his police. While I did this with my fingers, I took this paper out of his pocket. When we got down to the shore, none of the boat captains would take us across the lake. But I showed one man the paper, he read it and then he said, 'All right. Bring your people on board.' And we got across the lake. On the other side was America."

"And you got them out."

"Yes, I got them out." The claim is modestly made. "But you mustn't let on that you know about this," she says and looks sharply at me. "It would embarrass her."

The mother and daughter in this adventure are a couple she has met in recent years who have extended many kindnesses to her. Even to this day, the daughter, a grown woman with children of her own now, cheerfully runs errands for my mother to the library or store, and has been a regular and lively visitor at the nursing home. It is true that they fled the Nazis in France, for it is true that they are Jewish, and it is because they are Jewish that my mother cannot simply express her gratitude but must create this elaborate favor she did them, under the eyes of the SS Guard, and which they are only paying back with their different courtesies. Probably, they will never be able to pay it all back, because, after all, she had saved their lives.

My mother's job at the Bentley School started just as Hitler attacked Poland, and when she returned to Kansas City these days, her visits were full of endless accounts about her duties, the assignments she made. As I said, my parents had separated by now, so these academic reports substituted for the restaurant reviews we used to get. Moreover, these new stories were really for my grandfather's benefit. She rarely said anything to my grandmother and me if we were alone with her, but would idle in an impatient silence. She wanted to show my grandfather that someone was actually paying her money—a thousand dollars a year—for her intelligence, her education, and her ability. There, she could say; she was a success. But she would never be able to prove it.

As the war in Europe went on, her classes at the Bentley School began to fill with the children of refugees from Belgium and the Netherlands who had fled the Nazi blitzkrieg. They were well-spoken, she said, fluent in English and several other languages, and they were Jewish.

"Diamonds and emeralds as big as your thumb sewn into their clothes," she said. "Oh they know how to take care of themselves."

Moreover, and to impress her father even more with the tests she faced every day, she could tell—just certain things, you know—that alliances were being made between these new people and some of the other faculty. Miss Bentley, the school's founder and president, was a sweet woman but it was easy to see that she was being outmaneuvered. The atmosphere had changed.

Sometimes, after she returned to New York, I would lie awake in my room and imagine how it would feel to wear clothes sewn with precious jewels. Like chain mail maybe. And would they clink as you walked past customs, giving everything away? Such clothes would be uncomfortable but her other remarks actually did give me discomfort for a reason I could not put my finger on—for the time being. I ascribed it to a kind of class-consciousness, one student's resentment upon hearing a teacher speak harshly of other students. That my mother was the teacher made it all the more confusing.

Her efforts to prove herself to her father, then to her husband, and which these suspicions of collusion only made more valiant, raised an enclosure around her sensibilities that was to keep everyone at a distance—even me. Even her grandchildren. She sits in her wheelchair, isolated by much more than her great age—an aged Penelope, redoing memory to set things right and even the score. Justice will be hers if not freedom.

"So, you got them out," I say.

"Yes." She laughs, again, at how clever she was. "I got them out."

The women locked up in the prison on Sixth Avenue generally provide a last diversion for people leaving the bars after closing time. Mostly prostitutes, they have been rounded up for the diversions they have already provided on the streets and in the doorways of Manhattan, and they trade insults nightly with revelers standing on the street below, shouting obscenities and other pleasantries through their barred windows. The exchange is almost a nightly ritual, but I attempt to walk Tamar past the crowd on the street, mostly men, and to the Anglia parked near 10th Street. We have gone to Julius's earlier to hear some jazz.

But she pulls on my hand, and we stop. Some of the women shout down angry, vivid evaluations of the world in general and men in particular. Others get off funny observations that are cheered by the crowd. Some of the men shout up questions or add refinements to the curses raining down on them from the cell windows. One of the prisoners begins to sing and is joined after a bit, by another from two windows over, and this sisterly duet momentarily quells the rumpus. "Blue Moon."

Tamar's face is suffused with a kind of wry perplexity, the kind of look Sienese painters put on the face of the Virgin during the Annunciation. Her blonde lashed eyes are half-closed as if she's looking up into a flare.

On the walk over from Louis's, she's been very quiet, inward-looking, so I haven't disturbed her, haven't asked her about her husband. Perhaps, I don't want to know? But when we go on to the car and get into it, she tells me without my asking.

"His condition has stabilized," she says. "There might be some kidney failure."

"Should we change the reservations? Put them off a little?"

"No," she answers after a moment. I have headed the Anglia down Greenwich Avenue, going west. "Let's keep our date." She leans toward me and places her mouth over my right ear. "Once," she starts another story, and her wet tongue stuffs each detail into my hearing.

Even with a couple of years in the navy, and some time on a Washington newspaper, my sexual experience is mostly academic; that is, I have read more than I have done. But in the few days and nights I have spent with Tamar, my knowledge is becoming encyclopedic as one insight groggily follows another. More than once, just when it seemed a syllabus had been fulfilled, she would whisper in my ear, "Sometimes," or "Once,"—in a sultry hour before dawn—and a whole new course would be introduced that unaccountably would renew my scholarship. Dimly, it has sometimes occurred to me that I am in the company of a peculiar Scheherazade whose endless narratives are not so much saving her life but draining off mine.

In fact, Tamar has so distracted me that I have shot straight across 7th Avenue and now must continue all the way to 8th Avenue. I tell her to sit up and watch the scenery. Certain of her husband's specialties, like his desire to rip up new clothes, I cannot afford while others just don't appeal. I cannot bring myself to bite her pretty breasts as she has asked me to do a couple of times. But we have reenacted almost everything else the two of them had done in Ohio, which apparently is a much more worldly place than I have imagined.

When I make the turn at 8th Avenue, Tamar has slumped down in her seat and seems to nap. Further up, we will pass a bookstore on the west side of the avenue, just below Madison Square Garden, where most of my recent sexual research has been done. The window of this store is crammed with sun-faded manuals on carpentry and back issues of *Popular Mechanics,* but inside manuals of a different sort can be found; editions of classic erotica but all of them heavily censored within the proper limits of the 1950s. So, Aretino's *Life of Whores* is reduced to a flowery trivia; Nanna's advice to Pippa becoming nonsensical directions on pear cultivation; though, an occasional metaphor slipped the censor's literal scrutiny. That gentlemen sometimes prefer "the back of the book" is an index that Tamar has already opened to me.

In this store, one could browse between the missing lines of *Lady Chatterley's Lover,* Frank Harris's Memoirs and *Fanny Hill* and other similar editions, forced to fill in the missing scenes with one's imagination, or, to give that imagination a rest, leaf through art books that contained pictures of Hindu temple facades, archival photographs of Greek amphora, or the naughty bookplates of Aubrey Beardsley. Lots of hair and pinched faces.

A hardcover series called *American Aphrodite,* whose editor was to go to jail for public obscenity, offered reprints of the Kama Sutra, the tales of Bocaccio and Balzac and other curiosa that was in the public domain. The works of master engravers and artists accompanied these condensations. A timid selection of Giulio Romano's *Posizoni* fleshed out Aretino's poems, Rowlandson did *Fanny Hill,* and the austere prints of Fuseli popped up in a wide range of narratives. The prolific Perino del Vaga enjoyed a portfolio all by himself. Most of the Italian artists seemed more interested in the folds of drapery rather than the flesh within, and their lovers were heavy-haunched and often caught in a maneuver similar to a pair of draft horses making a turn at the narrow end of the field. In fact, as we cross 42nd Street, a few blocks from the store, Tamar has uncovered my caduceus, an exposure denied Mecurio because of all the bed sheets del Vaga wrapped around Glauros.

"I've got a test tomorrow," I tell her.

"In what?" she says after a little.

"Well, there's some disagreement as to when the -s plural came into Middle English. From the French, of course, but when? King Ethelred—known as 'The Unready'—married a Norman woman in 1002. Sixty years before the Norman Conquest."

"A Norman woman," Tamar says reflectively.

" . . . And that suggests French might have been spoken in the Saxon court before the Normans and Hastings. That she introduced the plural -s ending."

"That's the test?"

"It's an essay test," I answer. We have just passed the darkened bookstore. On the curb before Madison Square Garden, what looks to be maintenance and cleaning workers are waiting for a bus or a taxi. The marquee is dark. Joey Maxim and Bob Murphy have fought it out but are still on the marquee, and the clean-up crew has finished sweeping up the aisles, washing down the toilets and is going home. The Nedick's stand at the entrance looks even more disreputable in the gloom; how can anyone drink that stuff?

The most contemporary illustrations the bookstore offers are small, glossy black-and-white photographs of a model named Betty Page. These photos come in packets of a half dozen poses, neatly wrapped in cellophane, with a different picture of the series on top, so that the economy-minded browser can make a casual review of the whole set; perhaps on the way out of the store and after not locating the exact issue of *Mechanix Illustrated* he had come in for.

The photos show this raven-haired, sultry-looking woman in a variety of uncomfortable positions. She is sparsely, yet completely clothed in black underclothing with a black garter belt holding up black stockings. Her skin appears very white. She is sustained, if not suspended in these complicated *posizoni* by turns of small rope that wind around her ankles, her arms, and wrists to terminate in knots of a simple excellence only to be found in a Boy Scout Manual.

Moreover, the model wears glistening black pumps with heels of such a height that it is clear to anyone that if she had been able to break her bonds, she would not be able to run very fast. However, the expression on Miss Page's face suggests she has no desire to flee; in fact, she looks pretty indifferent to the whole business and in most of the poses, looks out at the camera with a bored insouciance, like someone waiting in line at the unemployment office. In a couple of shots she exhibits a startled moue of the mouth as if during some of the more strenuous arrangements, on a chair or over a table, she has let go with a little gas. In several others she looks down with a post-Annunciation tranquility, a passive acceptance of her complicated and highly stylized fate.

But we have pulled up across from my apartment building. Tamar is ready to complete the maneuver that del Vaga had drawn a bed sheet across. "Let's get a little sleep," I say.

"This exam means a lot to you." She dips her head a couple of times to agree with her own observation. The truth of it is new to her. And to me. Her near-albino stare looks puzzled, in the streetlights, a kind of bland appraisal. No disappointment, just the recognition of a fact. For the first time, she is really looking at me and she finds something amiss. Perhaps, she sees her predicament for the first time.

I cram for my test, as Tamar takes a long shower in the bathroom I share with several other roomers. She is a long time about it, for at this early hour of the morning, there is plenty of hot water, and so I have fallen asleep when she comes back to the room. I am half roused by the delicious aroma from her delicate limbs, like new-mown grass, and her fragrant skin is pink and ivory. I fall asleep with images of her guiding her sheep into mountain pastures. I can almost hear the innocent, atonal clang of roughcast bells.

She sleeps through the alarm and I observe her as I dress—one last possession. Her slenderness lies fully exposed in the morning light, the colors of her palette going from creams to rose save for her feet where the callused flesh has become an ugly orange. I tell her, I will be back with lunch and then lean down and kiss the blonde shadow of her triangle, a prospect, it seems to me, beyond any artist's rendering. She chuckles in her sleep, a knowing throatiness.

She is gone when I return. Today, the deli has given me lox as well as cream cheese, but she is gone. The new shoes have been neatly placed on the floor beneath the sink, and she has made up the bed. Pan American tells me the reservations have been canceled, but I could make others if I wished. They refuse to tell me if she has made another reservation in her name.

I have just remembered the title of that Chekhov story: "Dreams." Dreams realized can mock the dreamer, Zack had said the other night at Louis's. They can, to further employ his language, emerge from the dungeons of despair to create an unexpected tyranny. Look at Hitler, he had said. I am in Pittsburgh looking at myself going to Cuba in 1951, as I looked for a shortcut to being a writer.

Tamar had understood that I was not the Friday for her island, my footprints were to track on different sand. The cell of my room on 104th Street has become enormously empty and vast. I am pretty sure she has gone back to Ohio, back to her own imprisonment, leaving me to the dreadful freedom of the afternoon.

1993

Making It Up

My copy of *Robinson Crusoe* is an edition published in 1887 by Estes and Lauriat of Boston, and it was given to me by a man named George Iles on August 28, 1935. Mr. Iles lived a couple of floors above my father's rooms at the Hotel Chelsea, and he had befriended me as I rode up and down the hotel's rickety elevator—one of my favorite pastimes on those summers when I traveled from Kansas City to New York; when the season seemed to turn my father, mother, and me into a traditional family unit.

Hilary Masters from George Iles
with every confidence in his success
New York, August 28, 1935.

Mr. Iles's celluloid collars were of such rigid construction around his thin neck that I often expected his spectacled head to pop off like a cork from a bottle, but his formal attire in the elevator was a disguise for the bibliographic chaos of his rooms. Books. And then more books. He was a collector of books, and their jumble went from wall to wall and, to my seven-year-old wonder, all the way to the high ceilings. Laid up like bricks, the musty volumes formed a maze in which I could get lost as I inhaled the toxic fumes of their ancient bindery, become mesmerized by the embossed calligraphies along their spines. I walked through aisles of literature, and to this day my mind automatically puns his memory when I encounter the word. What I'm saying is that Mr. Iles provided me a stunning sensual experience, and though the transfer of knowledge upon innocence can become a scarifying episode, but sometimes with profitable consequences later as a dreary memoir, this Edwardian gentleman's seduction left me only eager for more ravishment; a normal life forsaken. Mr. Iles's gift of *Robinson Crusoe* made me a writer.

Back to my grandparents' house in Kansas City at summer's end, I came down with whatever infection was making the rounds of the second grade at Scarritt School. Let's say chicken pox. Quarantined to my bed and strengthened by my grandmother's oxtail soup and egg custards, my incurable boredom turned me to the brownish volume only just unpacked from my suitcase. "With twenty illustrations by Kaufman" the title page fraudulently claims, because there are no pictures and no evidence that any had ever been bound into the pagination, but my initial disappointment was quickly overwhelmed by the first sentence.

> *I was born in the year 1632, in the city of York, of a good family, though not of that country, my father being a foreigner, of Bremen, who settled first at Hull: he got a good estate by merchandise, and leaving off his trade, he lived afterwards at York, from where he married my mother, whose relations were named Robinson, a very good family in that country, and from whom I was called Robinson Kreutnaer; but, by the usual corruption of words in England, we are now called,—nay, we call ourselves, and write our name, Crusoe; and so my companions always called me.*

Whew! Talk about convoluted prose and cluttered punctuation! But the coils of language, the lassos of references held me face to face with several intriguing likenesses. *Though not of that country:* what country could I claim? Kansas City? New York? *My father being a foreigner:* my father was a strange figure to me, a mysterious man of puzzling importance who I only saw in summer. And to change one's family name called up a recurrent fantasy that I was an orphan and had been adopted by this kindly old couple who kept and fed me nine months of the year. The status of illegitimacy was not within my seven-year-old ken, but the sense of the condition was.

Moreover, the confident, first-person voice that speaks so casually and candidly from the page beguiled me. Trust and belief are immediately secured. I could hear that voice, carried it in my mind; a plain sound but sometimes with an offhand guile that tickled me with its timbre, a note later to be identified with irony. I was hooked and flipping through the early pages, their headings only drove the fluke deeper. "Misfortunes at Sea." "Captured by Pirates." "Escapes from Slavery." The man had a natural tabloid talent for grabbing a browser's interest. And these incidents some thirty pages before the famous shipwreck on the deserted island off the coast of South America and where my ultimate corruption procured by George Iles would commence.

But, in the meantime, Defoe's own story strikes out on its interesting own course. Perhaps, an excusable divergence here. It should be comforting to all of us who dare to write to know that this progenitor of the modern novel was something of a hack. He was born around 1660 (different biographies give or take a year), but almost thirty years after his fictional creation. He also changed his name of Foe to Defoe, thinking the Frenchified version had a little more class. Good for business. His father was a butcher who urged him toward the pulpit along with the fairly good education that went with the calling, but young Daniel wasn't called, preferring to set himself up in the hosiery business. In the seventeenth century, it's to be remembered, probably more men wore stockings than women, and the incipient author did well for a while, trading in Spain and Portugal, traveling through France, making it in London. Then, his business failed and he declared bankruptcy, but his political interests had been sharpening his quill in the meantime, eventually to change his course again as it was to affect our literary forms.

Born the year after the Restoration (Milton was still alive, blind and fuming), the ex-hosiery salesman pulled on a variety of opinions as a pamphleteer. He was enormously prolific—some count over three hundred tracts, pamphlets, and essays published under his name, not to mention the scads of journals he wrote for anonymously or edited. He somehow escaped punishment for his participation in the Monmouth Rebellion, but he did serve time twice and was even pilloried for his published opinions on religious freedom. He was convicted of libel once. His tracts ranged widely, advocating changes in highway construction, prison conditions, bankruptcy laws, and even recommending higher education for women. His ideas were usually far in advance of the period and often got him into trouble.

A satire called "Memoirs of Sundry Transactions from the World in Moon" is said to have given Swift the idea for *Gulliver's Travels* while *Journal of the Plague Year* amply proves Defoe to have been a first-class journalist. He had an eye for detail, he was a man on whom nothing was lost as Henry James might have said, but more times than not, his eye was on the mark, because he wrote for money, for advancement, and would take on any point of view that paid for it.

A satiric ode defending Dutch King William against the xenophobic whine of the Jacobites attracted the Court's attention, and Defoe was appointed the royal mouthpiece. While in this cushy post, he also wrote anonymous anti-Royalty pieces for the Jacobite journal *Mist*, but recent scholarship suggests he was serving as a double-agent in much the same way the CIA infiltrated the left-leaning editorial policies of the *Encounter* magazine in the 1950s. Nor did he neglect his domestic rituals, laying down his pen now and then to father seven children. He became very prosperous with a fine townhouse and a country estate but was to die in mysterious circumstances in 1731, having spent the previous year in hiding for reasons yet to be known. However, a dozen years before, in 1719, lightning struck him at the age of fifty-eight.

Or at least a meeting struck with one Alexander Selkirk, a sailor who had actually been marooned on a deserted island and who apparently handed over his journals of that experience to Defoe. No surprise that this classic of fiction is based on an actual event, hasn't that always been the case? Of course lately, the written life comes to us unadorned by invention, plainly out of the fire, uncooked if not unleavened and hastily served to appetites that prefer the dish not so much deconstructed as unconstructed. We seem to have lost the taste for reality put together piece by piece; perhaps a final counterrevolution against modernism's piecing, but that's another digression for another time.

So, this brief synopsis of Defoe's extraordinary life, some of which to be found in the introduction of my Estes and Lauriat edition, but prickly with chicken pox, I have no mind for it as I suffer confinement on Roberts Street. Especially because I have by now reached page 31, "The Ship Strikes upon the Sand." Here the magic commences, as does my apprenticeship.

The morning after the storm that has wrecked the ship and drowned his companions, Crusoe wakes on shore with only a pocketknife, a pipe, and a tin of tobacco. He swims out to the hulk, pulls himself aboard and starts to put together the reality of his next twenty-eight years, two months, and nineteen days. He begins to make new entities, fabricate items from a salvaged past. First a raft made of broken spars and planks to transport the usable stores he can find aboard the derelict. Corn grain that had been intended for the chickens that had perished. Muskets, powder, and shot. Some tools, clothing, rum and cordials—these last from the captain's cabin—this is all he was able to bring ashore that first day. In an irony for which we must credit Defoe, the ship had been on a slaving venture, so that its small cargo was composed of trinkets intended to trade with "Negroes" for other human beings—mirrors and strands of beads and such and all useless for a man trying to survive on an island. Except for crates of hatchets, that handy item of hardware for which many a tribe bartered away its land and existence. Crusoe brings off dozens of these.

The issue of slavery and colonialism hinted in these early pages and to be amplified in the person of Friday later can only be scarcely mentioned here to avoid a digression from the headway I'm trying to make. Because, in the meantime, Crusoe has made several trips out to the wreck, bringing back canvas sails, lengths of chain and rope, pens and ink, Bibles of both persuasions (but never to crack one of them), shovels, needles, thread—even the ship's dog swims ashore with him on the second trip as the crews's two cats gingerly cling to the bobbing raft. Bit by bit, he has assembled the materials to put his life together, piled them up around himself on this uncharted shore, all the ingredients for survival—to make a good story. He even creates more company for himself, in addition to the dog and cats, by training a local parrot to talk to him, teaching it to say, "Poor Robin Crusoe. Where are you? Where have you been? How came you here?"

thereby lending the bird a droll insight into the human dilemma it might not have come on if left to itself, eating nuts and berries.

Downstairs, my grandfather Tom Coyne rattles the glass panels of the bookcase and takes out a volume of the *Encyclopedia Britannica*—let's say Volume 7, "Damascu to Edu." But he's looking up "Diesel," not "Defoe," or maybe he's turning to "Dredging" or "Docks." This self-educated immigrant is obsessed by such research, and he glories in human invention, not the least his own. He had studied civil engineering by army correspondence school while riding herd on the Sioux, and he had put this minimal book learning to practical use building railroads in Mexico, Central America, and Peru. To read about the mechanics of human ingenuity and effort somehow reflected the picture of himself that he so vainly tried to hang in the American gallery.

For it was with such pieced-together knowledge and hard work that my grandfather confronted the hazards of this wilderness on whose shores he found himself at the age of fourteen, cut off from his family and his native Ireland. With no identity. Isolated. To say he coped would be an understatement though the word's primal meaning describes his constant struggle; a continuous setting up of defenses against the unknown and the unseen—even within his marriage and paternity. The continual preparation and repair of defenses is the life's work of the immigrant; it is a castaway's regimen even though an enemy may never show up. The labor of putting up walls, of making the fortress sound becomes more important than the fortification—even its purpose lost. Moreover, to erect a fortress around a property—even a picket fence—is to define the property and make it more valuable which, in turn, reflects upon the value of the work involved. Indeed, if no enemy threatens, the worth of the defense has been proved and the work of it justified. And its cost. Working hard is the success story of the alien—no other reward is really necessary, and, in any event, is rarely handed out.

The stakes and pales that the industrious Crusoe hews and pounds into the ground around his domain make such a fence, never to be attacked, though he fears the natives who occasionally barbecue their captives on one of his beaches. The first of these picnics is the occasion when he rescues Friday, but it is Crusoe who attacks the natives—a peremptory strike we might call it, slaughtering them with the instruments of his imported technology—the flintlock musket and pistol. But he is never satisfied with his security and constantly builds more fences, each new stockade enlarging his holdings, as if he doesn't have the whole island in the first place. It does not occur to me, at age seven, that the subtext of *Robinson Crusoe* is work, nor that this castaway shares the fear of being unrelated to his surroundings that all outsiders fear—like Tom Coyne downstairs reading the Encyclopedia. The construction an exile puts upon his reality not only is meant to defend the particular plot he has staked out, but acts as a sort of tether that keeps him from floating away from it.

But I do remember wondering why the man never took up fishing, a much easier source of food than the hardscrabble farming he threw himself into. A never-ending supply of food swam just offshore, but, of course, that would have been too easy. He planted and harvested corn, barley, and rice; learning how to conserve seed and manage his crops. He gathered and dried grapes to make raisins for winter meals. The wild goats that fortunately inhabited the place were domesticated for meat and milk. He even taught himself how to make butter.

Obviously, these are slim pickings, not the usual tropical island fantasy or the la-la land Odysseus sometimes washed up upon, but the isolated province of a philosophy that preached acceptance by a community, not to mention the Almighty, only came through hard work. Defoe surely carried the rigors of his Cromwellian youth, but the lesson was lost on me, my imagination awash in Defoe's quick-paced narrative.

The twenty-eight years plus pass in a couple of winks—one event comes fast upon the other. The guy could tell a good story, and he keeps the action moving, continuously. No modernist he, and the reader is given little opportunity to reflect or look around the narrative and wonder about time and space. Also, sensual details are totally absent, for Crusoe seems to have lost his appreciation for beauty along with his identity papers. He may look at the ocean, but it is to study its currents and tides, not to glory in its metaphysical splendor, and there isn't a single description of a sunrise or a sunset, and they must have been humdingers.

But that doesn't matter. I am caught up with the details of him putting his life together, as the story is put together, and my grandmother worries that I am straining my eyes. She's heard that certain childhood diseases can affect the eyesight, and in a way, she is right, for I will never look at the world the same way again. By now, the shipwreck has planted a large square post on which he notches the elapsed time of his abandonment. He invents a method that keeps track of weeks and months as well as days. His habitat consists of a reinforced cave and a second home for the dry season; a country estate if you will, made of the ship's sails. He's discovered how to fire the island's soft clay into pottery for storing grain and boiling goat stew. He's built boats and taken up tailoring, using the dressed skins of animals. He's rather proud of the jaunty cap he's designed and sewn together—just a little vanity left over from pre-Cromwellian times—so he's not a complete drab. He bakes his own bread, making up a way to grind the corn and sifting its meal and then putting together an oven from fired clay bowls heaped over with hot coals. He must do without yeast, but then he's not making Wonder Bread—the process itself is a wonder.

Once Friday runs pell-mell into his life, escaping consumption to become a factor of consumption, bells begin to ring in my fevered head. I had just read *Huckleberry Finn,* and that young exile's journey down the Mississippi, and with his own Friday, seemed very similar to the one I am reading, written two hundred years before. The raft that Jim and Huck shared was a sort of island set adrift, and they were left to their own resources to make do. To make up their identities. Surely, there must be a ton of theses somewhere on this likeness. But there is a difference. Twain backs away from the conclusion toward which his feelings are steering him, but his courage or his venality got him no further than the stunning metaphor for our national predicament, and maybe that's enough. But Defoe finished his novel with Crusoe continuing as the wandering loner, especially after Friday's death, to head out for the territories of China and Siberia, to return to England at age seventy to prepare for his "final journey," emphasis on *prepare.*

But another lesson has been teaching my imagination. I had already pictured myself as an orphan, set adrift nine months of the year from my parents; perhaps a prince forced into mufti. Kansas City was not quite a desert island, but something told me it wasn't where I should be. And here, in *Robinson Crusoe,* I came upon the plans and the methods to reconstruct my reality, to overcome my sense of isolation. Defoe was loaning me some of Crusoe's tools to create my own shelter and circumstance. The shipwrecked sailor showed me how to bring together scraps of happenstance—how the debris of the past and the present can be salvaged to make up a different identity, a new worth in the work of its own making.

1996

Disorderly Conduct

In jail in Worcester. It is February 1978, one week after the huge blizzard that has imprisoned all of New England, and I have just been locked up in a basement cell of the old police department on Waldo Street in Worcester, Massachusetts.

"What time is it? Does anyone know what time it is?"

The cry comes from a prisoner several cells to my right. I cannot see him. It must be about one in the morning, February 17. My son's birthday. A few hours from now, and about 120 miles west of here, his mother will wake him. "Happy birthday, honey," she will say. "How's it feel to be a teenager?" He is thirteen years old. But, I don't know what time it is because my wristwatch, along with my other valuables, has been deposited with the police clerk. A raw bruise made by the handcuff encircles my left wrist, where my watch should be—it took three cops almost five minutes to undo the bracelet when I was being booked. The arresting officer had fastened the handcuff.

"That's a little tight, isn't it?" I had said. The cop had pushed me face down over the hood of squad car to hook up my hands behind my back. The night was very cold and we are standing in a small arroyo of piled snow.

"I can make it tighter," he replied and squeezed up another notch on the cuff to prove it.

"What is this about?" I asked him. He looks very young and he is shivering though he had just jumped out of the heated cruiser. So, he's not all that cold. His partner, who drove the cruiser, is calm but sarcastic. "We do things differently here than in New York." He had checked my driver's license by flashlight. It is around eleven o'clock and there is no one on the street. This corner of Worcester is like some remote part of the Yukon—still and frozen.

The sixties have educated me as to how a badge can be worn by the wrong person. Nightsticks wielded lawlessly in the hands of the law. Selma. Greensboro. Chicago. I am thinking that there are no witnesses here on Main Street in Worcester. I had put up resistance, the cops could say later, and they had to use force to subdue me. They had not meant to kill me, but

I had kept resisting arrest. These things happen. I kept asking questions, so I was a wise guy. I had asked them for their names. Quinn and Germain. Quinn had cuffed me and, in doing so, became the designated arresting officer. He's only been on the street, it turns out, four months.

"Sometimes," my grandfather used to tell me, "they'd let a fellow go. Unlock the cell and say, 'Vamoose,' and the galoot would get to the door of the calaboose and they'd shoot him in the back. Say he was trying to escape." But that was in Mexico and in the time of Porfirio Diaz. This is Worcester, Massachusetts, in 1978, and I am terrified.

"What's going on?" I asked again. The hood of the police cruiser warms one side of my face. "What's this about?"

"Disturbing the peace," Officer Quinn replied and pulled me up and turned me around. They have called the paddy wagon to take me to jail.

Prison has been the ideal study for many writers; great literature has been created behind bars. At one in the morning I am calling their roll in order to take my place beside them. Cervantes, Raleigh, Dostoyevsky, Thoreau, O. Henry. Let's not forget de Sade and Genet. How about Mailer? Even Mailer was thrown in the clink. Jail is not such a bad life for a writer. All that I require is some paper and a pencil, and I can keep going. I don't need a seat on the toilet. I don't need shoelaces or a belt to hold up my pants. Just pass me paper and a pencil through the bars, along with the prison grub. Besides, I'm out of the weather; it's below zero outside. As for loss of liberty, a special freedom exists within enclosure. Restraint releases one from responsibility, from those duties imposed by the social contract, and the burden of normal relationships—even from a marriage going sour.

I should appreciate the irony of my arrest and embrace the opportunity of my imprisonment. Perhaps here in the privacy of my cell in the basement of this old building, I can finish the manuscript I have been lugging around the country for the last several years. I think of those happy monks of Clonmacnois, on the banks of the River Shannon, warmly cloistered and doodling, penning one illumination upon another to ignite the gloomy keep of their convictions. The family memoir I started three years ago in New York City, before driving west to Iowa to teach at Drake University, is almost finished. I have come to Worcester to teach at Clark University and have wound up in jail. And what's the difference? Isn't this stone cube with steel bars, with its marble slab for a bed, the ultimate retreat I have been seeking all these years—the pension I had thought to locate in academia? Moreover, here I will be given an identification, a number on my back, which might satisfy my wife's growing uncertainty as to who I am. "What is it you do?" my brother-in-law keeps asking. I have claimed to be a writer; yet my third novel was published seven years ago and despite the valiant efforts of my agent, nothing else has appeared in print. So to acquire some kind of identity, if not a little income, I have accepted invitations to teach, to be a visiting writer on campus.

But, now, I am just one more transient in this old lock-up on Waldo Street in Worcester, Mass. The building was designed by George H. Clemence, a local architect, and completed in 1918. His design is a compact example of the Renaissance Revival popular at that time. The four-storied pressed brick facade is ornately trimmed in terra-cotta with rondelles and foliated windows; so, by day, the building resembles a wing of the Ufizzi that has somehow been detached and relocated in this old industrial city in central Massachusetts. The basement jail is saturated with authentic Renaissance odors.

But, this is the middle of the night, so I cannot appreciate Clemence's genius from this low vantage point. Nor had it been my choice to visit this landmark in the first place! "Enjoy the trip, Professor," Officer Germain had said as I was lifted up the rear steps of the paddy wagon. Had Holy Cross been my host institution, the officer's attitude toward me might have been different. "What are you doing in Worcester?" Officer Germain had asked, looking at my New York driver's license. He had ignored the rest of the identification I offered him, brushed it aside; membership cards in the Authors Guild and the American Society of Magazine Photographers. These cops are like my brother-in-law.

"I am a visiting faculty member at Clark University." The campus is within walking distance.

"Where are you going and where are you coming from?" the younger cop asked.

"I'm going home. My apartment is just around the corner. I'm coming from a party near the campus."

"Have you been drinking, Professor?"

Two drinks. The party had broken up early. I have answered calmly, aware of the sarcasm growing in their address. *Professor.* I put my mind onto something else. I had been doing research yesterday in the Clark Library on James Audubon. His wife's name was Germaine. With an *e*. Briefly, I fooled with the idea that Officer Germain might be related. Should I ask him?

In the sixties the Clark campus had acquired a reputation as a haven for hippies in contrast to the orthodox environs of Holy Cross, or the serious turf of Worcester Tech, or the respectable halls of Assumption College.

But, in fact, all four of these schools have invited me to Worcester. Rookie Quinn's father, it turns out, is a lieutenant on the force, and his son, who seems ready to shake apart with anger, must have grown up hearing mealtime stories about the pot-smoking, rock-scored anti-war demonstrations at Clark—the live-ins and love-ins. And here I was, I could almost read it on the young officer's face; here was the current transgressor-in-residence of public morality standing before him on the corner of Main and Allen Streets at about 11:30 at night.

The four schools had gone together to form the Worcester Consortium for Higher Education. Their purpose was to pool funds and facilities and invite writers to their different campuses; each hosting a writer for a semester where he or she would work with students selected from the four institutions. In the fall semester, Galway Kinnell had held poetry seminars on the campus of Holy Cross.

"How do you like it here?" I had asked Galway. Earlier in autumn, I had driven over from my home in New York to attend a reading he gave on the Clark campus. Another part of the job was that Consortium writers were to give public readings of their work at different locations around the city. But to say Galway gave a reading is not a fair description, for, as is his practice, he recited his luminous poetry with almost no reference to the printed page. Several years back, a mutual friend had introduced us, and now we were having a beer, after his presentation, in a bar near the campus.

Galway did not answer me directly. Having grown up in Pawtucket, Rhode Island—part of the greater Providence—the mill town atmosphere of Worcester might have seemed familiar to him. The ramshackle nature of the place, its depression and falling-down was a character similar to how I remembered Pawtucket from my own time in Providence at Brown University. The industrial exodus after World War II to the South had retreated through all of New England. We also share a friendship with Stanley Kunitz, and Galway mentioned that Worcester is the older poet's birthplace. He thinks Stanley hasn't been back to Worcester since he left for Harvard some fifty years before. I got the feeling that Galway didn't spend a whole lot of time here himself—maybe, only showed up for his class at Holy Cross.

"What are you doing in Worcester?" Officer Germain might have asked Galway Kinnell.

"I am a visiting faculty member at Holy Cross," he would answer.

"Ah, Holy Cross, is it," Officer Quinn might have said. "Here, can we give you a lift to where you're staying? It's a cold night and the streets around here are full of suspicious characters who teach at Clark."

But where is Galway Kinnell while I am in this jail? Send for Norman Mailer! Get me out of this place! Today is my son's birthday, and here is his father, sending him good wishes from behind bars. I may seek the cloistered life, but I want some say in it, a choice of imprisonments.

"There's probably been a mistake," the booking sergeant said. He's a trim, dapper guy with an Italian name, and he's been casually observing the struggle the two cops are having with the steel cuff on my left wrist. My hand was growing numb. The sergeant's manner suggests a tolerance of all-human folly and depravity. He's seen it all. Therefore, my innocence must strike him with the force of an April sun. At last, he steps down from his desk and lends his own expertise. The steel bracelet falls open with a blessed relief.

"You're damned right there's been a mistake," I said. "A terrible mistake."

My arrest on the corner of Main and Allen Streets was so obviously a mistake, that the sergeant's regret has been made even more acute by the knowledge that he must continue the procedure; he has no other choice, his manner suggests. He is as much a victim of the process as I am. Sadly, he must lock me up until the district court meets in the morning where—not a smidgen of doubt on his face—justice will be done. But in the meantime, he'll just change the charge from *Disturbing the Peace* to *Disorderly Conduct*. The silent, wide-eyed chorus of cops around him maintains such a fix on their Celtic moon-faces that I almost do the laughing for them.

Just like the movies, I'm allowed to make one phone call. A policeman pokes through the change I've just handed over for safekeeping, and hands me the proper coin. The pay phone is mounted on the wall of a corner in the station house, above a broken-down sofa that has been shoved into the space beneath. In order to use the instrument normally, I have to lean on a seat cushion. "Get your knee off that couch," a voice commands. I stretch and dial the operator and place a collect call.

My wife is delighted that I have called her for a chat at this hour. She starts talking about our son's birthday, the plans for the party, which I will miss. I have to cut her off, and as I talk through her amazement, I am aware that I have become the focus of the station house's midnight improvisation. We are all in it together, cops, my wife, and I, taking up our different parts and reading our lines. I am letter perfect; a careful rendition of the outraged citizen whose innocence has been impugned by the cruel destiny that hailed me at the corner of Allen and Main Streets. I can feel the eyes of the chorus behind me lift to heaven. My wife gasps and something like respect edges her voice. Perhaps, I have surprised her with recklessness, daring she had never suspected.

But I need help. The only person I know in Worcester is the chairman of the Clark English Department—the man who hired me. "Call him and tell him to get me out of this place," I tell her.

Jonas Gilman Clark founded his university in 1889; about ten years before another self-educated, self-made millionaire industrialist, Andrew Carnegie, set up his own alma mater in Pittsburgh. After success as a carriage maker and a manufacturer of general hardware, Clark left his native Worcester in the 1850s to go west to California where he made a fortune selling supplies to gold miners. Then came the Civil War with its entrepreneurial opportunities, and these profits were turned over and further compounded by his canny investments in government securities.

Meanwhile, Mr. Clark had also accumulated an enormous private library. He also acquired acreage along Main Street, about a mile and a half from where I am about to be locked up, on which he built a university in 1889, and where   some ten years later—the terms of his will established a near separate institution given to the undergraduate study of the humanities rather than a graduate curriculum of the first school. If only Clark had given the place a more practical twist, as had Carnegie with his advanced trade institute, night classes for blue-collar workers and homemaking courses for their wives, I might not have been handcuffed and given a trip downtown to this Italianate dungeon.

"I am a visiting faculty member at the Clark Institute for Serious Mechanics and Useful Engineering," I could have said to Officer Quinn. A sudden warmth in his eyes would have thawed the icy bond between us.

In 1909 Sigmund Freud was lured from Vienna to Worcester with the promise of an honorary degree (plus $750) from Clark to address a mammoth congregation of world famous psychologists, put together by the university's president, himself an eminent psychologist. William James showed up "just to see what Freud was like." Also on the panel were Freud's protégé and associate, Carl Jung and, during this meeting in Worcester, the two men deepened their suspicions of each other that were to widen into the schism that marks the practice today. About twenty years later, physicist George Goddard joined the Clark faculty and fired off the first liquid-fueled rockets into the atmosphere. So, onto this launch pad of explorations into both inner and outer space, came this vagrant, unheralded fiction writer in the winter of 1978, looking for a space to make his own.

The Clark English Department had reserved a dormitory room for me, perhaps Kinnell had been offered similar accommodations at Holy Cross, but I wanted a space with a kitchen and a quiet corner where I could set up my typewriter. I had already begun looking for such a place several years before—a retreat from wife and children in which to do my work and pursue the illusive persona I wanted to be. The surroundings were not all that important; a cave, a tree house, or an island like Crusoe's. How about a cell?

The small apartment on Benefit Street had one room, kitchen and bath, situated on the top floor of a dilapidated building a half dozen blocks from the Clark campus. The previous tenant had left with the front door lock, knobs and all, so my first order of business was to acquire and install a new set from a hardware store. Next was to get a bed, since the landlord-agent's interpretation of the term "furnished" did not include this appointment. I gave up my appeals and made up a palette on the floor of my duffel bag stuffed with towels.

The chairman of the English Department, the same man my wife is waking up at midnight with the news that I am in jail, had greeted the descriptions of my apartment, especially my sleeping arrangement, with respectful awe. Clearly, my hardy pioneer spirit impressed him. Since Jonas Clark's day, the neighborhood around the Clark campus had badly deteriorated into a ghetto of the poor and the deprived, the miserable and the dangerous. But the atmosphere strangely appealed to me, and in fact I lived in a similar area in Providence, while attending Brown. Curiously, the street name was the same—Benefit.

My traveling typing table fit neatly into a corner of the small kitchen which was self-contained and snug like the cabin of a tidy sailing craft anchored in a protected harbor. The blizzard that raged outside shook the warped windows to sift small strands of snow upon the stained carpet. I was warm and dry and typing, and, in a way, Clark University was paying me to do this typing. The seminar students were alert and superior. My mornings and most of my afternoons were free. The resources of the university library turned up landmarks in my family's history, a geography that had been largely unmapped territory for me. I have been trying to revive my grandparents and my father so they might explain themselves to me; justify their movements across that old landscape where I had been abandoned. And, without intending to, I was seeking a reunion with my mother; at least on paper, piece together an understanding of her careless love.

So, in these squalid rooms I knew the transcendence all writers can experience. I was able to leave my hovel on Benefit Street and enter the abundant fragrance of my grandmother's kitchen in Kansas City or I could climb onto my father's lap and drowse through a summer afternoon redolent with the odor of his sweat and the hazing of insects in tall weeds.

But outside, it was a different atmosphere. The callous, uncaring attitude of absentee landlords was evident on every street corner. The waste of their expedient greed encrusted every stair landing. Roaches and rats carried the messages of their indifference. Tenants were abused and cheated and their citizenry insulted by the presence of slow-moving police cars, armed and armored as if they had been manufactured for the civil wars of Central America but had somehow taken a wrong turn and wound up here in Worcester. In this neighborhood. Their continuous patrol of the streets became not so much an enforcement of its safety, but an enforcement of its residents—looking out for disorderly conduct. Or so I began to feel.

What I am saying, is that when Officers Germain and Quinn stopped me on the way home from this party, a presumptuous anger has already proselytized my mind. I have put the discovery of my own abandonment, while incidentally abandoning my own family, together with the alienation I presumed on my neighbors' behalf, to make a false and self-serving alliance. After all, in the pocket next to my indignation, I carried the other half of a round-trip ticket, which could take me out of these demeaning conditions. I was white and mobile. I could simply get into my car and drive two hours due west, across the border to New York, and to the relief and refreshment of the old farm that my family and I have set up as our own private preserve. I have been arrested for all the wrong reasons, but that's not unusual.

Meanwhile, my wife has wakened the English Department chairman to tell him the writer he has hired as his contribution to the Worcester Consortium for Higher Education has just been thrown in jail for disorderly conduct. She is to tell me later that he was incredulous, but that he knew just the man to set it right; just the person to get me out of jail. This person was a faculty member who directed a program, funded by the U.S. Justice Department, which was supposed to raise the consciousness of the Worcester Police. In fact, this professor helped the Chief of Police get a masters degree. So, as the steel-barred door of my cell slides shut with the clang of a closure by Poe, buttons are being pushed for my release.

Perhaps Officers Germain and Quinn had suspected in my movement down Main Street a whole array of crimes that I had got away with up until then. Disorderly conducts. To claim that as a description of most writers' lives is a disingenuous plea at best. In the basement of Mr. Clemence's handsome building, I face the wall and multiple accusations.

I have deserted my children; not physically so much as spiritually and emotionally, committing the same desertion that I am trying to write about. Is this the same pattern that has begun to appear in the matter of abuse? Do the abandoned grow up to abandon? But the court will not permit irony. What are the extenuating circumstances? There are always extenuating circumstances. My purpose had been to make myself into a father worthy of their respect and love. In the meantime, their wounds have been deep.

More misconduct. I have lied to my wife. I have cheated on her. After more than twenty years of marriage, I have been disloyal to her in an affair with another woman. Could I plead the extenuating circumstances of a marriage gone stale? Of career and marriage going in opposite directions? An old story, a likely story—surely, the judge will turn a deaf ear. How would a jury of peers, picked at random from the neighborhoods around Benefit, find me? They would probably conclude that I had been picked up just in time.

"What time is it? Does anyone know what time it is?" my fellow prisoner down the cellblock has just cried out.

About four hours ago, I walked the half dozen blocks from my apartment back toward the Clark campus and to the party that was given in my honor. A welcome to Worcester party. My tall farm boots crunched the snow of the narrow paths shoveled like a maze through the towering drifts. The frigid air pricked my nose with every breath. So, the warmth and buzz of fellowship that spilled over the rooms of the large apartment warmed more than my bones. My host's girlfriend, it turns out to be her place, must have stuffed mushroom caps all afternoon. The platters were piled high. Plates of cheeses and meats, bottles of wine and whiskey; the buffet was more than ample. Moreover, local writers, most of whom had never heard of me, have been invited. My host's introductions vouched for me—he was a colleague at Clark. A couple of journalists were also present, including Ivan Sandorf, the former book editor of the *Worcester Telegram and Gazette*. He said he vaguely remembered one of my novels. So, passing from the subzero temperature outside into the glow of this candlelit reception, I pass through a kind of checkpoint. My papers have been found all in order—my identity has been verified. Headiness pumps through me though I have only had a single bourbon and water.

Maybe an hour later, I notice that both host and hostess have disappeared. Others also begin to wonder about their whereabouts. Neither has been seen at the buffet table. Nor in the kitchen preparing more treats. The bathroom is unoccupied. The party is coming apart, and people are running out of things to say to its unknown guest of honor. During an awkward calm in the conversation, we hear the sound of flesh striking flesh. The slaps are answered by cries that resemble the yowls of a cat whose tail has been stepped on. Pain or pleasure, we cannot tell which, but the sounds come from behind a closed door of a room across the central hallway of the apartment.

The party is glued in place by a fast-drying perplexity; a mixture of concern and amazement is fixed on every face. Then, one of the guests suggests we leave and give our hosts some privacy. She seems to know about their habits. Their unusual conduct has brought the party to an early end, and I am once again out in the cold. I bid good-bye to my newfound audience and start walking down Main Street toward the rendezvous with Officers Quinn and Germain at the corner of Allen Street.

The huge piles of snow pushed up by bulldozers resemble temples abandoned by a vanished race. The storm had been so enormous that army tanks had been brought in to clear the runways of Logan Airport in Boston. The pale, incognizant blink of streetlights cast a bluish patina over the deserted street that resembles an Arctic necropolis. But a block from my corner, a glow of life reflects upon the snow. The ground-floor windows of the Bancroft House of Health Care, a nursing home, are outrageously illuminated. Signs of life!

These windows are partially blocked by the snowdrifts. Their venetian blinds have been pulled up, and in the first window, as I pass by, I can see two people sitting on a couch. One is a registered nurse, wearing her cap, and both women are studying something at their feet. In the next window, as I have moved along, are a man and a woman who also look down at something below my line of vision from the sidewalk. What's going on? What has commanded this total concentration? My journal is in a side pocket of my parka, and I am prepared to be both witness and chronicler of any human event that comes my way. I walk up to the front door, beneath the porch light, and lean to the right to look through the second window.

Just as I suspected—it's an emergency! Someone's breathing is being restored. A man is bent over the body, doing mouth-to-mouth resuscitation. But it is all in vain, because it is a dummy being worked on and I am witnessing a class in CPR. My journal notes contrast the sober expressions of the humans with the merry whimsicality molded into the dummy's face. I note the unreal redness of the plastic figure's wig. All of this observation takes a few seconds. Then, I turn around and continue on my way, walking in the street for the sidewalks are still blocked with snow.

At the next corner of Allen Street, the police cruiser pulls up beside me, nosing in toward a snow bank to effectively confine me. The two police get out. My lawyer is to speculate later that if the older, more experienced Germain had been in the passenger seat, he would have got to me first, and my arrest and imprisonment would probably not have taken place. But Germain was driving, so it was the younger, inexperienced Quinn, the son of a lieutenant on the force, who got to me. I was his.

Immediately, I knew why they had stopped me. They had been cruising south on Main Street and seen this suspicious character standing on the porch of the nursing home, wearing boots and a parka with the hood up, peering into one of the windows. If I had been at the wheel of the cruiser, I would have turned it around myself to come back and ask a few questions.

So, I told them what had been going, what I had been observing. I suggested we all walk back and look in the window together to see what was taking place on the floor of the home's recreation room—to verify that I hadn't been spying on old ladies and gentlemen preparing for bed. They weren't interested though they are to testify later that they did check out my story, but only after I have been hauled away to jail. I answered all their questions, handed over all of my identification. I was coming from a party, I told them.

"Have you been drinking, Professor?" Quinn asks sarcastically. His pale face seems to have thinned and he trembles, maybe from the cold. Germain has taken my driver's license and gets back into the cruiser. "What's going on?" I ask. "We do things differently here than in New York," he says. They have closed the doors and rolled up the windows. I am left in the well between the car and the snow bank, which towers above my head.

"Do you remember what the temperature was?" my lawyer will ask Officer Quinn at the trial.

"It was quite cold."

"And it was about eleven o'clock at night?"

"Yes, sir," Quinn answers.

"Where did you leave Mr. Masters when you and Officer Germain got back into your police car and closed the doors?"

"Beside the cruiser."

"Did you leave him standing between the snow bank and the cruiser?"

"Yes."

"Did you invite him, on this very cold night, while you were conducting your investigation, to sit in the cruiser with you?"

"No."

"Was the cruiser warm?"

"*Yes, it was.*"

"*Having been informed that he was Mr. Masters, that he was on the faculty at Clark, that he was on his way to his apartment, which was only a block away, that he had a valid license, you nevertheless left him stand in that cold temperature between the snow bank and the cruiser while you got into the police car to do some further investigation?*"

"*That would sum it up quite well,*" Quinn responds.

"*At that time you had placed him under arrest?*"

"*No.*"

"*Up until that point, you hadn't felt that there were any grounds, at least, for charging him with disorderly conduct?*"

"*At that point, no, sir.*"

Then, several moments later, my lawyer is to ask, "*By the way, Clark University has its own police department, doesn't it?*"

"*To my knowledge, it does.*"

"*And it has a campus police?*"

"*Yes.*"

"*With full powers of police on campus?*"

"*Yes.*"

"*Did you use your radio to contact the campus police to come to the scene?*"

"*At no time did I contact the campus police,*" Quinn will say.

I was a suspect, and their manner scared me. Who I claimed to be was of no importance to these police. They had ignored the cards of membership that supported my claim to be a writer and a photographer. "What is it you do?" I could hear my brother-in-law's question on the night air. I seem to get arrested in Worcester for looking in the window of a nursing home. "Why don't you get a job?" my wife would ask. I'm trying to find a job but these cops have interrupted the search and left me standing outside in the cold on the corner of Allen and Main Streets. In fact, they have taken my driver's license and got back into the cruiser. After a couple of minutes, I edged myself up on the fender of their car and pulled out a book from my parka. I had bought the book just that afternoon, and, using the glow of the streetlight overhead, I began to read Susan Sontag's *On Photography*.

"*Humankind lives unregenerately in Plato's cave . . .*"

The doors of the police cruiser burst open.

"Why did you sit up on that police cruiser?" my lawyer is to ask me during our first interview. He has a modest office on Harvard Street and his name is Richard Welsh. At this point in our relationship, I know more about him than he does of me. In the early morning hours after my eventual release into the custody of the Clark faculty member, I had phoned a former classmate who was practicing law in D.C. Les Hyman in the 1960s had been the chairman of the Massachusetts Democratic Party; so, he had a book almost on everyone in the state, especially lawyers. Obviously, this is a connection not available to my neighbors on Benefit Street, but all the more reason that I use it—on their behalf, I tell myself.

Les Hyman's book on Welsh notes that he is a Greek and Latin scholar who taught these subjects in high school as he worked his way through Boston College. Therefore, he is a Jesuit-trained and full-fledged Roman Catholic, important credentials for Worcester. He is the father of a large family. One child studies music. But most important, my friend tells me on the phone, is that Welsh is not from Worcester and has only recently established his practice in the city—he's yet an outsider and has not been brought into the cozy establishment that informs the local court system. But he is savvy on the local bench. And one more thing, Hyman adds, Welsh pumps iron on weekends.

"So, tell me," lawyer Welsh asks, "why did you sit on that police car?" Welsh is a stocky man with thick shoulders and a round Irish face. Even sitting, he seems to barely contain a lean energy.

"I had this book, and I didn't know how long they were going to take." He is looking away, bored. "And it was cold," I continue. Welsh looks back, getting interested. "Well, I guess I was just mad."

"Right!" He leans forward.

"And I was tired." His eyes are smiling. He waits eagerly for me to go on, to give him the right answer. "And there was no place I could sit down."

"Okay." One hand slaps the top of his desk. "Here's what I'm going to ask you on the stand, and here's what you're going to say. Mr. Masters, why did you sit on the fender of that police car? And you're going to say that it was your way of expressing a *mild* protest at the way you were being treated by the police."

"A mild protest."

"Right. The First Amendment of the Constitution covers such protest. The Mass Supreme Court just reaffirmed this interpretation in a case. Remember, a *mild* protest." Then he shrugs and smiles good-naturedly. "Of course, this probably won't mean much in the District Court but when we appeal that verdict to the Superior Court, the plea will carry some weight."

"It will? We're going to appeal?" The wheels of justice have already run over me, but not to worry. We're appealing.

"Of course," Welsh says. "The District Court judges always listen to the cops' side. You'll get a guilty verdict, but then we'll appeal."

"We will?"

My advocate's eyes appraise me, evaluate my qualities as a client. Somehow the nature of this interview has been reversed. Finally, he says, "What does your freedom mean to you, Mr. Masters?" I've been seeking that answer for several years. In New York City. In Iowa. Now in the frozen streets of Worcester. Should I soil his clear-eyed, Jesuit view with my equivocations— my freedom at the expense of wife and children, the use of that freedom and the dubious value of the results? Welsh doesn't give up, and he gives the question an objective turn. "How much is an American citizen's freedom worth?"

"I was only in jail a few hours," I say.

"Ten minutes or ten years—it's all the same. It's all the same if you're unjustly imprisoned." He is lecturing me. He could probably say it in Latin, and I see him addressing the old Roman Senate, a little bulky in his toga, as he rises to defend this vagrant Celt, a peddler of romances. He's the right man, but, first, I have to get out of jail on the morning of February 17.

Which I am more than ready to do when the keeper shows up at my cell with his bunch of keys. It's a little after one in the morning, and I am no more satisfied to be holed up in this underground writers' retreat designed by George Clemence. I've admitted my crimes, pled guilty to desertion and adultery, arrogance and selfishness—hubris in the first degree. Now it was time I was released. I've been punished enough so slide back these bars.

The envoy from Clark University has arrived, and I am led upstairs to another part of the police station, the main lobby. Here, the faculty member who helped raise the consciousness of the Worcester Police greets me, and he turns out to be the genial host of the party I had left only a few hours before. He is very much at home in the station, calling officers by name, being greeted by others; hugs all around. My arrest has precipitated a jolly reunion. "Hello, Sarge," he says to one. "How's the wife?"

Meanwhile, the young woman whose unique martyrdom had caused the early break-up of the party, and which had put me on the fateful course toward Officers Quinn and Germain, waits on a bench on the far side of the room. She seems composed, her shapely legs crossed and one foot idly marking time, but as I approach, I note her pretty face looks swollen from crying. When I sit down beside her, she takes a few ragged breaths and hiccups a sob or two, all of which I take to be a residue of the particular ecstasy that my arrest may have interrupted. "It's okay, Ruby," I say, patting her knee. "It's okay," I repeat, feeling that the injustice done me has stretched out to include her as well. The man who should be arrested stands free at the high desk across the way, trading jokes with a couple of policemen.

The sergeant sitting at this desk waggles a couple of fingers at me, and I approach. "Before court this morning," he says as he signs my release paper, "go to the Probation Office. It's just down the hall from the courtroom. Go see this guy." He writes the name on a separate slip of paper. "He can do something for you that will save you money." My host nods agreeably. He's worked out a deal for me—I have been given back my freedom because of his influence.

But I am not entirely convinced. On the ride back to Benefit Street, I watch and listen to my benefactor and his girlfriend from the backseat of his car. They chat cheerfully about my experience, how it was a terrible mistake and that it would all be over in a few hours. Everything would get back to normal, they both agree. But can I trust their definition of normality? On those classic scales that Justice holds, how far down must one side sink to raise the forgiveness or the approval of another? In human love, perhaps a similar formula is to be worked out, one that makes for a continual immolation of the heart. Montaigne would have speculated on these roles we play—the demeaning positions that we sometimes have to assume in order to enjoy an ephemeral freedom.

But it is nearly three in the morning, and I must not digress. When I get back in my apartment, I call Les Hyman, wake him in Washington, D.C., and ask him if he knows a good lawyer in Worcester. Hyman has also instructed me to ask for a continuance, a postponement, when the court convenes at eight o'clock in order to engage a lawyer. But, first, I look up the guy in the Probation Office recommended to me by the desk sergeant who had signed my release papers. The guy who can save me money.

This officer is peeling off the lid of a very large plastic cup of coffee, a burning cigarette stuck in one corner of his mouth. He looks like he's been up all night too, and, in fact, he already knows all about me. The folder with all the particulars of my arrest are on the countertop before him. He sips the coffee carefully, almost delicately, one pinky finger stuck out, as he opens up the thin dossier and reads. After a couple of swallows, he says, "There's nothing here. It's all a mistake."

"You're damned right," I say.

"Court convenes," he pauses to check his watch, "in half an hour. I have something for you that could save you money."

That phrase once more. Certainly, the system is admitting that Quinn and Germain were out of line. The system recognizes my innocence, and

I'm being offered a deal that would save me money as it saves face for the system. How often, I wonder, has this alternative been used to settle such mistakes? How many mistakes have been made?

Meanwhile, he's been explaining the offer. In return for my tacit admission of guilt, made right now in the privacy of this office, I would be granted a "nonverdict" that would disappear from my record once I completed a probationary program of group therapy. He shrugs, as if to say that, in my case, this last requirement would probably be waived. I wouldn't even have to attend the sessions. His eyes fix me with a bleary collegiality—it's a simple, easy solution to the problem Quinn and Germain had put all of us in a few hours before. Just sign this paper, on this line. Simple.

The nightmare looks no different in the hurtful light of day, and I am exhausted. Yet, something makes me hesitate. An alarm works through the cotton stuffing in my head. Off the record or not, I will still be pleading guilty to a misdemeanor I have not committed. Most of my life may have turned on misdemeanors, my whole career a docket of disorderly conduct, but I had been a cold, cooperative, and solid citizen at the corner of Main and Allen Streets. Moreover, Welsh is to tell me later that the deal offered me is a probationary program designed for juvenile first offenders—to give kids a second chance. Obviously, I fulfilled none of those requirements.

At this point in my journal, the entries spill over the pages with a righteous scrawl. My response before the weary probation office was no less idealistic. How could I face my students, if I signed this? What of my honor? My integrity? What would I say to my children? It was my son's birthday. Is this the sort of gift I should give him—his father copping a plea? I did not offer my neighbors in the ghetto, but, I thought, if I accepted this offer, wouldn't it be to desert them once again? But, the guy has already closed up my folder and turned away, taking an exhausted drag on his cigarette. He walks over to a file cabinet. He has done all he can to help me and to no avail. A sad case. It's going to cost me money.

Whatever majesty the law is supposed to have, the quality was absent that morning in the Worcester District Court. A comical version of Balzac by way of the Marx Brothers was in progress when I took my seat at the rear of the courtroom. I spotted Quinn, already there and in full uniform; truncheon and pistol holstered in the leather harness buckled around his waist. But for now, both accused and accuser become temporarily unified, a single audience for the acts being brought before the judge sitting at the front.

The accused seemed to be unnecessarily trying out for roles for which they have already been cast. The vagrants and prostitutes, the petty thieves and the others charged with conduct that had offended the City of Worcester and the Commonwealth of Massachusetts during the night might have been giving auditions, not so much to win roles but to garner evaluations of their performances in them. The district judge enjoyed every one, winking and nodding and smiling to convey his pleasure with the artistry of the pleas thought up by the different wretches who stood before him. "That's a good one," his affable shake of head suggested to the court clerk and the sergeant of arms who, in turn, relayed to the lawyers and the police and the rest of us the measure of this particular strolling player's routine. "Thirty days," the judge announced and cracked the gavel. The clerk rose to introduce the next act.

Quickly, in a matter of only two or three cases, we become aficionados, experts in the law and the tradition of this District Court. This particular judge. Critiques were exchanged—one verdict compared to another. This performer had dropped a line or looked away at the wrong moment. Missed cues were unforgivable. "Six months!" The gavel smacked down. The guy got off easy, someone said—for Christ's sake, he'd waved his hands like he was selling vegetables. The gavel raised and lowered on the next bad behavior. A performance so poor that the judge had to hide his laughter behind his hand. The rest of us were embarrassed for the condemned. She should have worked harder on her lines. "Detained for psychiatric examination." Bang!

I had begun to enjoy the burlesque myself, laughing out loud at some of the egregious excuses offered for a moment's indiscretion, a fall from civic grace. Sometimes, cops would double over, thump each other, in shared amusement. The court stenographer had to interrupt her record to wipe her glasses and her eyes. One actor said he hadn't known his wife had closed their bank account when he wrote and cashed that check at the McDonald's he managed. Here's a good one, someone whispered. The man's story was eloquent, full of modern complexities—corporate insensitivity, a woman's revenge, how circumstance can suborn the best of motives. It was a tale grounded in contemporary angst and the place was riveted silent. The judge's face had grown long and his eyes turned heavenward. Then, *bang* went the gavel. "Six months in the workhouse, full restitution, plus damages." It had been a socko performance!

"The Commonwealth of Massachusetts against Hilary Masters."

The call lifts me to the ceiling where I expect a yardarm to suddenly appear, and I am Billy Budd. All the crimes against family and myself pull me to my feet, and I want to shout out—to join all those condemned creatures who have preceded me—"Yes, guilty. I am guilty! Hang me. Better to be punished for the wrong crime than to go free of the others." But, of course, I ask for a continuance and it is granted.

"We're hiring our own recorder," Welsh tells me a month later. We're about to go to trial on the charge of disorderly conduct brought by Officer Quinn. "The tape they use in the District Court sometimes gets erased." His look is of forced innocence. "This way our person will be sworn in and her record will be official. So we will have an exact transcript. For the appeal, you know."

In the meantime, advice has not been scarce. My wife had wished that I had taken the option, the plea-bargaining. Her brother had just been appointed to a minor political position in his hometown, and he hoped things could be kept quiet, for he suddenly had ambitions of his own. An older writer friend advised me, "Stay away from lawyers—read Dickens!" My lover, in New York City, patiently listened to my late-night phone calls, and then assembled a complex of moral principles for my infantile indignation to climb. Not so much justice but her continued favor waited at the summit.

We've had a change of judges too; not the merry hangman I had witnessed the morning after my arrest, but an older judge because the court calendar had become overcrowded. "The verdict will be the same," Welsh assures me reasonably, "but it will be pronounced more pleasantly. This judge thinks of himself as a gentleman."

"But I will still be found guilty—pleasantly guilty."

He nods agreeably. "Then we will appeal to the Superior Court which will have a jury. We will probably win that one. Then, we sue them?"

"We sue them? The cops?"

"You want to do that don't you? You're still mad, aren't you?"

"On what grounds?"

"False imprisonment. Malicious prosecution. Assault and battery." He holds up the color Polaroid I had had taken of my bruised wrist at a shop that did passport photos the day after my arrest. The flesh has since healed and shows no injury.

And everything else *has* gone back to normal, as I had been promised it would. My manuscript was almost finished. I had sent off a portion of it to Houghton-Mifflin for their new work contest, and they had asked to see more. I never mentioned my arrest to my writing seminar at Clark, but I think the students knew anyway; perhaps the colleague who had freed me had passed the word. Actually, both he and the department chair seemed a little perplexed, as my wife had been, that I had not taken the probationary deal. That I had hired a lawyer seemed to worry them also. How is it going, they would ask, a little distance in their voices. This visiting hack in residence was about to compromise the university's reputation. The Worcester Consortium for Higher Education was going to be dragged through the papers. Why hadn't I just played along and accepted the deal?

In his testimony, Officer Quinn said that I had "climbed to the top of the snow bank and jumped onto the hood of the cruiser." The snow bank had been over my head.

"How did he land? asks Welsh.

"He landed on his behind," Quinn answers. I am watching the judge. His aristocratic features are solemn, not a flick of incredulity, not even a little amusement.

"He didn't jump with his feet on it?" Welsh persists.

"He didn't land on his feet, no."

Welsh asks Quinn to estimate my height and weight, and he makes guess—about six feet tall and 170 pounds. Then, *"Did he do any damage to it?"*

"Not that I know of."

"Did you look?"

"I checked it. I could find no damage," Quinn answers.

Welsh has paused and looks for a long second in the direction of the bench. He is asking the judge how a man of my size and weight could leap from a high snow bank, ass-first, upon a car hood without damaging it. Not even a dent, his glance insists. The judge looks down at his notes. Yes, yes, he nods impatiently. Let's get on with the hanging.

But, as it turns out, Officer Quinn and the Commonwealth never had a chance. Both were represented that morning by an inexperienced law student, working as an intern in the Prosecutor's Office. Perhaps, the authorities were confident the system would take care of itself, that the procedure required no more experienced hand to steer it toward a guilty verdict. Or maybe, they just didn't care or, not all that familiar with Richard Welsh, they underestimated his Jesuitical yen for justice.

For another reason, I had already begun to feel a little sorry for Quinn earlier that morning. I had been waiting for Welsh in the small coffee shop of the courthouse before the court convened. The young officer appeared in the doorway, almost timidly, looked around and then walked to a table in the center of the room where a group of policemen, Germain among them, sat talking and having coffee. Like Quinn, they were in uniform and waiting to give testimony on the charges of their arrests, but there the similarity ended. Quinn had pulled up a chair and sat down on the edge of the group.

He leaned forward, alert to pick up the subject of their talk, to laugh as they laughed—to be part of the group. His eagerness to be a member of this company of seasoned officers seemed to vie with his insecurity in that company. A light clicked on in my head.

As the son of a lieutenant, he carried an extra integer on his badge number. This questionable credential, like an eleventh fingerprint, would always put the performance of his duty under a special review. The men sitting at that table, chatting easily among themselves might be skeptical of his very presence in their ranks because of this chance of biology. His awkward hankering to press himself into their fellowship, that caused his laughter to be just a little too loud, was familiar stuff to me.

My own father's fame and image has often been invoked by lazy or spiteful reviewers of my work. I have been judged and found guilty of an unsought nepotism—for even having the temerity to be published. The verdict, after a dozen books under cover, is still being handed down, and I wonder if the same is true of Quinn all these years before. He might be a lieutenant himself on the force today, but perhaps some of his colleagues yet sentence him to this peculiar confinement, this prejudicial judgment of his talent and ability.

When the manuscript I was trying to finish in Worcester finally found a publisher three years later with David R. Godine, Donald Hall wrote a wonderfully insightful review for the *New York Times Book Review* that commended the prose and the structure of this family biography, and he particularly singled out the way the figure of my mother emerged as the book's central character. Of the four characters in the book, both the mother and the grandfather surpassed the "father figure" in importance. He was only one of four characters. Yet, an editor on the book review, ignoring Hall's account of the book, falsely characterized the memoir. EDGAR LEE MASTERS WAS HIS FATHER the headline above the review proclaimed.

More recently, my second collection of short stories, *Success,* gave the anonymous reviewer on *Publishers Weekly* the chance for some cheap psychological analysis, spending most of the space to advance a theory of my supposed competitive relationship with the poet of *Spoon River* and how that relationship, obviously, influenced the title of the collection. As for the stories, they were barely mentioned.

Ivan Sandorf, the former book editor of the *Worcester Telegram,* has been called to the stand to testify on my behalf. Welsh questions him about my behavior at the party. Was I under the influence of alcohol when we all left at 10:30 the evening of February 16? No. How had I behaved? Like a gentleman. A key word in that courtroom that morning. Earlier, Welsh had asked me the question we had rehearsed in his office, "Mr. Masters, why did you sit up on the fender of that police cruiser?"

"Because I wanted to make. . . ." some kind of protest, but what kind? On the stand, my mind had blanked out, and I couldn't think of the qualification Welsh had told me to say. The Supreme Court had said a citizen could make some kind of protest to his treatment by a policeman. It was covered by the First Amendment. But what kind was it? "I wanted to make a . . . *gentlemanly* protest to the way I was being treated."

Not the right word, but Sandorf told me later it had been very effective. Looking on from the courtroom, as he waited to testify, he said the judge's head had raised slightly and, with a smile, he had scribbled on his notepad. "Right then," Sandorf told me, "I knew you were home free."

And so it went. Welsh's acute questioning, Quinn's inconsistencies, together with the student prosecutor's inexperience began clearly frustrating the judge's desire to find me guilty. "Where is your case?" he finally asked the other lawyer. "Where is there the substance that I can use to find for the Commonwealth?"

"Well, your honor," the young lawyer answered. "If the police cruiser had been called to a scene of an emergency when the defendant was sitting on it, he would have constituted a hazard to public safety." The judge had begun shaking his head halfway through. No, no, he said, and with a light tap of the gavel, he found me not guilty.

But I was guilty as charged. My conduct had been more than disorderly. I had been fleeing the scene of many crimes when temporarily stopped at the intersection of Main and Allen Streets on the night of February 16. My rush toward that freedom, and the validation I hoped to find within it, had collided with a similar urgency of Officer Quinn's. He proved his worth squeezing an extra notch on the handcuff around my left wrist, giving me the chance to thumb my nose at all those who had questioned my identity, who had not accepted my credentials. Revenge is a cold supper.

The morning has become clear in Worcester and the air fragrant with the earth's warming turn toward spring. Richard Welsh and I stand on the steps of the courthouse. The city of Worcester seems to be laid out before me. "Now it's our turn," he says and his eyes are merry.

1993

About Hilary

For about thirty years, I had my given name pretty much to myself. "Hillory born early this morning," my father noted in his diary's page for February 3, 1928; later adjusting the spelling for my birth certificate after a review of family records. The first Hilary Masters was born in western Virginia and fought in the Revolution; afterwards to move his family to Overton County, Tennessee. "There's a whole hillside of Hilarys in Overton County, Tennessee," my mother would often say to people who asked about the unusual name as if the magnitude of this plantation would justify if not explain why such a name was given to a little boy.

So, even my mother may have felt funny about the name, but she was from Kansas City, Missouri and, also, she had only been given the choice of my middle name, Thomas, from her father.

Growing up in Kansas City, and especially the northeast section of that river town, I was made aware of my name's uniqueness early on. It singled me out at school and in my neighborhood. If my grandparents had lived in the tony southwest section of the city, my name would probably never have been questioned, never raised an eyebrow in the fashionable by-ways of the Country Club Plaza. But, Hilary? "Isn't that a girl's name?" No, I would explain it was not, sometimes citing the hillside in Tennessee as proof; that is, if there was time before the wrestling match began and a few wild punches thrown. Eventually, most of my school chums modified this foreign handle into a nickname that was more comfortable for them to use—Hil, which several close friends call me even today.

But in the meantime, I was the only Hilary on the block, maybe even in the world outside of Overton County, Tennessee. Once I ran across some books in my father's library by a Hilaire Belloc who was obviously a French guy who couldn't spell. Then, in the late thirties and early forties, I became aware of a beautiful blonde actress named Hillary Brooke who played mean, conniving women on the screen of the Chief Theatre up the street and around the corner, on Benton Boulevard. As the war in Europe came nearer, she also did a couple of aristocratic Nazi spies, but the role that impressed me most was that of Rochester's haughty and aloof fiancée in Orson Welles's "Jane Eyre." Hillary Brooke made a dazzling entrance, I remember, that shrank drab Joan Fontaine down into her Mary Janes. Later on she became the foil of the zany Ritz Brothers—a kind of Margaret Dumont to their emulation of the Marx boys.

So, this was my first encounter with a woman using my name, misspelled as it was. But, I told myself, in Hollywood no one went by his or her real name, and I knew all about stage names. Even in Missouri we knew that Cary Grant was not really Cary Grant. Obviously, this actress had taken my name for its different sound and because it seemed to go with the upper-class characters she usually portrayed.

Only a few years later, in 1949, the integrity of the name was restored for me when I saw the statue of my patron saint on the side wall of the Madeline Cathedral in Paris. Unquestionably, this grandfather of all Hilarys was definitely a man. St. Hilary (or Hilaire as the French insist on spelling it) was born a pagan but died a Bishop of Poitiers after defending orthodox Christianity against the heresy of Arianism which suggested that Jesus was a supernatural being, a crossbreed of the divine and the human. Hilary's birth is figured sometime around 320 A.D., and he grew up in Bordeaux, then the intellectual capital of Gaul. Arianism had the backing of the Imperial Court in Constantinople, the Eastern Establishment of that day, and because of his eloquent attacks on this belief, Hilary suffered banishment and exile which, eventually, was to earn him his sainthood.

He wrote hundreds of polemics, a dozen books or more, in a Latin that some have ranked with Boethius for style and graceful expression. He was "a trumpet of the Latin tongue," his contemporary St. Jerome said in a contemporary review, "famed for his eloquence wherever the Roman name is known." However, some said Hilary's style was convoluted, too many "Greek flowers" as one wit cracked, but these critics have lone gone to their rightfully anonymous dust in the dark vestibule of the man's brilliant history. Triumphant and free in his last years, Hilary returned to his bishopric in Poitiers to introduce his flock to congregational singing, even writing the hymns for them to sing and thereby becoming the first Christian Latin hymn writer.

Here, indeed, was a man and his name was Hilary. A man of action, a man of principle, a man of letters, and—eventually a saint!

But, about when I came across the Medieval playwright Hilarius (circa. 1127) in a university lit course, I had begun to sense a change, like the subtle shift of seasons that would raise up the old challenges all over again. Some acquaintances announced the birth of a daughter—Hillery. Another little girl, Hilory, was reported by a newspaper to have accompanied her parents on a visit to the Grand Canyon. The Rhode Island spelling bee was won by a fourth-grade schoolgirl, Hillary—who had defaulted before she had even opened her mouth; I wanted to tell somebody. The name began to pop up everywhere attached to scores of girls, and, like all conspiracies, the initial signs seemed unconnected to the onslaught that was to come.

As far as I can figure out, sometime in the late forties and through much of the Eisenhower era, a peculiar frisson rippled through the maternity beds of America, all carrying the name *Hilary,* and its various spellings, into the minds of mothers-to-be in the same way maybe as the spores of ferns are carried by a forest breeze. It is a common phenomenon, how certain names like Kelly or Candy or Bruce become the fashionable nominative of a generation. Or maybe these mothers had seen the same movies I had and had been impressed also by the strong, independent stride of Hillary Brooke across the screen. In some parts, she even wore riding boots!

Whatever the reason, it was becoming clear to me that few, if any boy babies were being tagged as Hilary while the woods were full of hundreds and hundreds of *hilaria femina*. It was like a natal zeitgeist had run its current through these expectant mothers in the later forties and early fifties, and I suspect some of this same charge may have crackled through Mrs. Hugh Rodham of Chicago, Illinois, as she waited to give birth to her daughter.

So having fought and won the good fight for my identity on the northeast side of Kansas City, I found myself challenged thirty years later in the effete, but no less deadly surroundings of the East. At cocktail parties, people hinted my parents might have made a mistake, or some, with more analysis under their belts, suggested my father and mother had tied me to this obvious female name as a deliberate but curative "wounding." The less witty, at beach cookouts, opined that the obstetrician hadn't looked closely enough or—even more cruel—perhaps there hadn't been all that much to see. But I was good-natured, even though it was apparent that by now thousands of young women were using my name. I was fair-minded, saying that the name was "epicene," though I doubt this, but the term froze the glib smiles and glazed the eyes. The more learned recognized my generous willingness to share my name, a gift across the genders you might say. Let them not only have a room of their own, but take my name as well. That sort of thing.

My tolerance was to be even more confounded when Gloria Steinem and company put the title *Ms.* into our culture and onto envelopes and the labels of mass mailings. As this title addressed the pejorative distinctions some women experienced due to marital status, or the lack of it, the term unexpectedly included me as well within its palliative. Would Ms. Steinem, I wondered, be comfortable with the thought that she had put a male under the same cover with thousands of young women?

Because the thousands and thousands of women who by now bore my name of Hillary or Hilery or Hillory began to receive their mail addressed as *Ms.* The secretaries or addressing machines saw the name coming and *automatically* used the prefix without giving a thought that the recipient just might be a male descendent of that hillside in Overton County, Tennessee. But feminists might have appreciated one error, for it may have illuminated the sort of prejudice the use of *Ms.* was meant to address.

About ten years ago, my application for a Fulbright came back with a letter of regret addressed to "Ms. Masters." My response was both swift and Holmesian. Look at my application and the supporting materials and references again, please, I asked the administrator. Clearly, he and his colleagues could not have addressed me as a woman if they had read even the first cover letter, which refers to me as a male. I had been rejected out-of-hand, perhaps, because I was thought to be female. The return letter of apology was enforced by a promise to review my file, and they did review it—and I did receive a Fulbright. I was sent to Finland in midwinter.

But gradually, through such corrections, and the efforts of my publishers, my identity as a male was being restored. True, there were probably millions of women by now bearing my name but a faithful and even growing audience saw my image on the bookflaps of my books and recognized me for what I am. Reviews of my work referred to me in the masculine possessive; some even called me, *Mr.* Masters. Of course, an occasional lingerie brochure might slip up and the Policeman Benevolent Association, in fruitless phone appeals for funds (they always asked to speak to Ms. Masters who was never home) didn't get it; yet, the situation seemed to have stabilized. Those restless spirits on that hillside in Tennessee rested easier. I had learned to live with this minimum level of confusion, and the fad seemed to be over and those of us who could draw a breath, drew it.

Then, in 1992, disaster struck in seventy-two-point headlines. And, to think that I voted for her husband, in what must have been a kind of unconscious act of self-mutilation. She has renewed all the old controversy and confusion with every issue of the *Enquirer,* with almost every editorial in the *New York Times.* Think of the millions and millions of pregnant women sitting in doctors' waiting rooms, leafing through issues of *People.* The consequences stagger the mind—only Carl Sagan could grasp the dimension. Some may think the situation hilarious, but my identity has been compromised, and sounds of woe rise from the South once again.

1994

Passing through Pittsburgh

The Greater Pittsburgh phone directory lists 191 numbers under the family name of *Coyne,* and there must be other households of that name that are not listed or who may not have a telephone. Not exactly in the same league with the Joneses, but yet a sizable Irish colony which may explain why my grandfather showed up here around 1875 at the age of fifteen, his first stop on a trek toward a citizenship that always seemed to elude him.

Tom Coyne, his brothers, and one sister all immigrated together, having walked from their village of Leenane west of Galway City to Queenstown, or Cork, where they took the boat for America. Whispers in family archives gossip a melodramatic flight from British authorities due to the body of a priest found pitchforked on the family sheep farm. This was the time of "the tithe" and the younger Coynes' father, Black Phillipe, was supposed to have had enough of the ecclesiastical rip-off, whether by the Roman Church or the Church of England. So, the story goes, they were on the lam and someone may have said, "You have cousins in Pittsburgh, Pennsylvania. They'll take you in." But they all split up once coming ashore in the New World, further suggesting they were running from something, and, in fact, when my grandfather made his only return to Ireland at the age of ninety, he tried to get a passport under an assumed name. He might still be wanted, he feared. Whatever, he was the only one of that family to come to Pittsburgh, and he was vague about his time here in 1875. It seems he was only passing through.

Carnegie, McCandless and Company had been founded by 1873 and the Edgar Thomson Steel Works in Braddock had already installed the first Bessemer. Frick's coke empire was underway; glass making was a close second to steel as an industry in this boomtown where one could feel "the actual physical presence of power," to use the words of a contemporary *Wall Street Journal* article.

Tom Coyne must have breathed the power of the place, felt the heat and rhythm of its industry. The great number of steamboats and barges on the rivers probably impressed him for they served the largest inland harbor of that time. He was fond of such assessments; the largest *this,* the greatest *that,* the most powerful *other,* maybe because he was a small man himself, wiry and resilient but with a Celtic fury in his eyes to compensate for his stature. After his army career, his life would be fitted to heavy machinery—locomotives, the great locks of the Panama Canal—engines to cross and move the earth, divert oceans. Along with the river vessels, the six railroads that focused on Pittsburgh must have firmly centered this fascination.

And in all probability, he arrived in Pittsburgh by train, coming from Kings Point, Brooklyn, where he landed—this some twenty years before Ellis Island—to Philadelphia and then Pittsburgh. Just two years before, in 1873, the train trip from Philadelphia to Pittsburgh had been cut down from twenty-five hours to only twelve—what better proof to this young immigrant of the powerful society he thought he had joined? The place fired his sentience for human invention to a white-hot fervor that was never to cool.

Why didn't he stay? "The mill work was too much for me. I wasn't strong enough for it." But he was strong enough to break and handle cavalry horses only a couple of years later. Strong enough to construct railroads all through Mexico and Central America. In Ecuador, he built and ran the railroad from Quito to Guayaquil—an arduous construction that crossed the Andes. In his seventies, he was strong enough to disarm two muggers in Kansas City, send them fleeing and to capture one when the man fell over a fireplug. When the police showed up, they found Tom Coyne kicking the thief's behind. He had to be restrained. So, it wasn't that he was weak or fragile, but for some other reason he got back on another train after a year or two in Pittsburgh and headed west. He was a Connemara lad and perhaps there were aspects to Pittsburgh, with all its industrial wonder, that were too much for him. Or not enough.

Some years later, I am going by train in the opposite direction, and I am eight years old. My mother and I have taken a Missouri-Central from Kansas City to Chicago where we changed to a Pullman sleeper on the Pennsylvania Railroad. The next morning, my father will meet us at the Pennsylvania Station in New York and we taxi across town to Grand Central where we get on a train of the New York Central's Harlem Division that will take us, on a roadbed laid down in 1852, to a small town near a rented farmhouse in Columbia County. The whole trip will take the better part of two days and a night. It is a summer pilgrimage I was to make many times to fulfill my parents' peculiar concept of a family, for my grandparents kept me nine months of the year.

This particular trip east occasioned my first look at Pittsburgh, and it was a sleepy look from beneath the blind of my Pullman berth's window, but it was a sight that burned into my remembrance. Midnight or early morning, the train's scheduled arrival in Pittsburgh is unknown to me, but it is pitch dark. Some change in the train's rhythm has awakened me. I snuggle down in the cozy cave of my upper berth—no bed linen will ever match the crisp luxury of Pullman sheets—they had the cool freshness of a fine memory.

Nor, if I may switch onto a little sidetrack, has the special effect of train travel been matched by any other form—something's been lost. Train travel permits a passenger to encounter others in a different space, poses a relativity between object and viewer which Einstein fully appreciated. These days we mostly travel cut off from the world we traverse, only our destination and arrival time are defined. But to pass by train through a countryside, to take up temporary residence in another place, and to intersect, however briefly, with other lives waiting patiently at a road crossing, that particular human experience has been all but lost, and I think the human imagination, without this free association, has been impoverished.

But, here I am, entering Pittsburgh at eight years of age, on a Pennsylvania Pullman to New York City, coming up the Ohio River, McKees Rocks on the right, then into that cut through West Park and across the Allegheny at 11th Street into Daniel Burnham's gorgeous terminal, erected to replace the old depot that was burned down during the 1877 railroad riots. The riots would have occurred a couple of years after Tom Coyne came to town.

I raise the window blind, and, still drugged with sleep, look out on a scene that Turner could have painted. Violent explosions of color, of whiteness. Billowing clouds of fire blossom from the dark to metastasize into orange and scarlet plumes. The sun is coming apart. I am terrified and fascinated all at once, as it is always awesome to look into the center of power. My mind's camera was permanently marked with this image of the mills turning common ore into iron and steel, making something new out of the ordinary—an immense, catastrophic breakdown and reintegration.

Tom Coyne must have had a similar view. The particle residue of coal fires clogged the air, not just from the mills but from the city's fireplace grates. Perhaps, my grandfather warmed himself on cold winter mornings at one of these narrow grates; let's say, staying with a Coyne cousin. He never said. So, I am free to wonder. Maybe he didn't hit it off with the relatives— personal relationships were not his forte—so, he might have rented a bed in one of the many rooming houses that boarded single men, mill hands, and perhaps in one of the row houses of my neighborhood on the Northside in which the floor planks of yellow pine still show the old nail holes that marked off those cramped corners which transformed a normal-sized living room into a crowded dormitory.

Surely, he might have thought, this was a paltry citizenship he had exchanged for the fresh air of Connemara, the dew of Galway still upon him. For these grimy alleys he had left the clear streams where trout fought for a place on the hook. For this gritty domain, he had turned away from the long vista of Killary Bay where salmon entered to spawn and Viking ships had once ghosted on a westerly breeze. It may have been this mystical perspective that pulled him away from Pittsburgh, and not the hard work, for his whole life was one of hard work, and it would be too clever a hindsight to suggest that he objected being separated from the product made by his hard work, and with borrowed tools at that, or that he felt himself made expendable—dross to be burned out to make more efficient fuel. Those ideas were around then, of course, but he never thought that way. No, I think those mythical images he carried from Ireland pulled him away. He tried to duplicate them on the coulees of Montana, in the jungles of Central America and the heights of the Andes. Then, there were those riots of 1877.

The management of the Pennsylvania Railroad, the same company that had brought him and me through Pittsburgh at different times, had decided to do a little downsizing in 1877. Trainmen's salaries were to be cut 10 percent; moreover, freight train lengths were to be doubled thereby reducing the number of jobs as well. The city rebelled. Burghers blocked the tracks. Mayor McCarthy refused to call in the police, and the members of the local state militia would not raise arms against their neighbors. Under pressure from the railroad company, Governor John Frederick Hartranft called up the militia quartered in Philadelphia, and after arriving by train, these men assembled, confronted the citizenry and, on July 21, fired into a crowd, killing twenty people. All hell broke loose. The mob drove the troops out of Pittsburgh. Over a thousand freight cars were demolished and nearly a hundred and fifty locomotives were destroyed. Dozens of downtown buildings, including the depot, were burned to the ground. The city was brought to a halt, to the edge of total anarchy, and it was the most violent uprising in America since the Civil War—not to be equaled—if then— until the riots of the 1960s. I can understand how it might have discouraged my grandfather. How was this oppression of a citizenry any different from the history he had just left? Exchange the Pennsylvania Railroad's board of directors with Queen Victoria's cabinet, and it looked like the same sort of tyranny he had learned to hate at his father's knee. It had been waiting for him here, in Pittsburgh. And the air was bad too.

Something else to conjure. Almost exactly a year before, on July 4, 1876, George Armstrong Custer led the Seventh Cavalry to its destruction on the banks of the Little Big Horn River. The battle had made all the papers.

The stupidity of Custer's foray was glossed by the glory of his death, for his opponents this time around were not the old men, women, and children slaughtered at Washita and Sand Creek but were—as my grandfather was to say later—"the greatest light horse cavalry ever to go into battle." So, it was something like a fair fight, and in the clean, open air as well. He even might have been cheered by the Sioux victory; the underdog had won this time, and though he was to spend five years in the U.S. Cavalry, his sympathies were always with the Indians. The irony was not lost on him that to gain his own citizenship, he had to suppress and diminish the citizenship of others. This awful paradox would sometimes make him weep.

So he left Pittsburgh. "I worked on the railroad," he would say when asked how he got to California, and that was all he would say. The Irish laid a lot of track, going east to west, as the Chinese did from west to east. Unskilled labor, such as a mill worker, was about all that was available to him in a society that discreetly placed signs in its windows: *No Irish Need Apply.* "Sometimes I was called a white nigra," he told me once, and the confusion still welled up in his pale blue eyes. Yes, the comparison offended him, but also he was outraged that men, African or Celt, should be put into such an equation at all. In San Francisco, he enlisted in the U.S. Cavalry at the Presidio: five years' service would give him citizenship, at least on paper, and these were to be "the happiest days of my life." He was assigned to the Yellowstone whose trout-packed streams and the clean air reminded him of Connemara, and where he witnessed the American Indians' harmony with nature Their way of life would become a lifelong paradigm.

But what looks smooth to me this morning on Monterey Street was actually a disjointed record. We make such narratives to iron out the discontinuity of our lives, give tumbled events a cause and effect—even a reason they may not have possessed. The endeavor comforts us as it helps us believe that we were, in some way, in charge of the past when it was happening—a condescension as much a folly. Though this behavior might explain the myopic affection we have for the past—worked into sweet nostalgia like a piece of leather until it is soft and supple to our self-appraisals. Worked on until past events come out right. We prefer unity in these revisions, everything under one roof so to speak, and the piecemeal configurations of the original smoothed over. Card players illustrated by Norman Rockwell pleasure this nostalgia—the same game pictured by Cezanne can scare the hell out of us.

So, I admit to a certain lack of control of this material, and merely to put the different parts of my life and my grandfather's life, and Pittsburgh, into a pretty cohesion will only be my arbitrary arrangement of the bits and pieces. The particles themselves will remain unaltered and unexplained and the inquiry unoccasioned—an idle amusement and nothing more.

However, two years after my first passage through Pittsburgh, I came through once again but this time by plane. My grandfather gave me a round-trip ticket to join my parents via a Trans Western Airlines DC-3 which stopped to refuel in Chicago and Pittsburgh. The flight took over six hours, about the same time it took Tom Coyne to go from Philadelphia to Pittsburgh, and I mention this commonplace only to recall his exultation when I became part of this proof of modernity, a passenger on this demonstration of human invention. My grandmother was more of a traditionalist and apprehensive of all gadgets, especially those that lifted a person several thousand feet into the air. "I can see his little legs dangling through the clouds," she said worriedly.

I enjoyed the trip, pampered by the stewardess with extra helpings of chocolate cake, chewing gum, but the time spent on the ground in Pittsburgh draws a blank. Unlike that other early morning passage, I can call up from memory no views of the steel mills, no clouds of fire and smoke nor even a trace of the rivers' fork. Moreover, we landed far outside of town at the old airport. The plane's altitude and flight path separated me from these city marks so my memory is left holding an empty contour, but I was distanced from more than a place.

Back on the ground of this Pittsburgh where I live, a similar separation from place, from a past meant to nourish the present, has been happening here and in all American cities the last half of this century. It goes by such names as Urban Renewal and Cultural Renaissance, and it is a process born of the suburban mentality that has always lived outside a city's limits and is uncomfortable within the rough edges of its neighborhoods. So, bulldozers are called in to smooth the awkward edifices of the past; selected artifacts installed in museums to be viewed safely on weekends.

My own neighborhood had been a part of Allegheny City, an independent urban entity across the Allegheny River from downtown Pittsburgh. Fifty years ago, the five hundred buildings of this commercial center were torn down and replaced by a mall—that vulgar pastoral of suburban zeal. Today, this mall is all but empty; a derelict of corrupt planning because the local populace had been isolated by its very construction, separated from their natural thoroughfares and haunts. Most of these places have been obliterated and major streets truncated.

To build the Civic Arena, home of the Pittsburgh Penguins, fifteen hundred black families were made refugees in their own city and neighborhood. Perhaps there is a connection between this displacement and a finding that puts this city at the top of the list for having the greatest number of impoverished African American families. Cut off the circulation in a hand, and it becomes numb, useless, and it is the same with a neighborhood. Cut off the flow of its inborn traffic, and its citizenry are diminished. The place rots. Perhaps, city people should beware of suburbanites seeking, if not bearing culture.

Lately, a so-called Cultural District has been marked off in the center of the city and designed for attractions that will lure culture hounds from the glens of Fox Chapel and Sewickley. But how can culture be segregated, and is it wise to do so? Culture is diminished when set apart from the community that is supposed to inspire it; indeed, from which its own inspiration is drawn. It becomes legal and bland. This current undertaking is merely another mall that will market the national chains of entertainment enterprises; fuzzy reproductions of Broadway boilerplate and the weary appearances of celebrity *artistes* on the road. It is more than a passing irony, that the "renewed" area previously hosted the city's prostitutes and porno dens, agents of another kind of veneration that was also set apart from the community. But vice has always been segregated—now, in Pittsburgh, it seems to be culture's turn. At the same time, I would guess that in the neighborhood bars of Bloomfield, Homewood, and the South Side, more genuine, spontaneous culture (neighborhood myths and local heroes remembered) is celebrated on any night of the week than in a whole season of imported attractions in the glittering halls downtown.

Tom Coyne, in his quest for citizenship, wanted to join the power of Pittsburgh. He wanted to contribute his energy and invention to that power, but he had to move on, because he found the power was exclusive, misdirected and made harmful to the very people it was supposed to enhance, to amplify. My search for identity is neither as desperate nor as direct; after all, I am second generation, and I can afford to loaf a little on the banks of these three rivers. But I am no less mindful of the struggle for identity, for a place on this river delta; so, in the temporal coincidence some call history, Tom Coyne and I are merely passing through.

1997

My Father's Image

This morning in Villefranche sur Mer, a low layer of nimbus covers the harbor, softly chased by a discrete sun. Beyond, Cap Ferrat stretches out to enclose the *rade* like the arm of a sleeper, and just over its shoulder of pink roofed villas clustered in pine woods lies the village of Beaulieu where Chekhov visited in 1897. A black schooner loafs on its mooring below. Today is my birthday.

I think I must be the same age, sixty-eight, as my father was in the picture that just arrived by fax from a publisher who asks my permission to use it in a school text. The electronic transmission has bleached out all the textual subtleties of the original photograph so he is barely on the paper. Only the circles of his glasses distinguish the roundness of his head, and the ghost of his torso rises into the space of blank paper where the black trapezoid of a necktie floats unattached. My fading remembrance of him must fill in the slant of shoulders, the muscular arms, though perhaps my eyes have been fooled as memory is always shaded by nostalgia.

He is seated, a hand silhouetted against the book it holds, and I am standing beside him. I look to be about six or seven, though I am dressed much older—made up like a miniature adult and probably for this picture session. I also wear a necktie that has become, in this reproduction, a striped missile, and my left hand curls into a half fist against the dark swatch of long pants—a nervous, uncertain gesture perhaps fetched by the unfamiliar scratch of material against my bare legs. Or maybe it was the formality of this moment of record that bunches my fingers; possibly being posed beside this man, my father, who I rarely saw and hardly knew. He seems to be regarding something outside the picture.

Yet, the overexposed quality of this reproduction has left the remains of a smile on my child's face, though the dimples we both share have become invisible. My head is slightly turned down and toward him, a sketchy cant of affection, even a curious interest, emphasized by the shadows of my boyhood's long eyelashes. This morning on the Cote d'Azur, my eyes strain toward a second sight, no more to be trusted than any other, to fill in the blanks left by an indifferent electronic signal and generate the feeling in that room of the Hotel Chelsea, that summer's day in, let's say, 1936.

Almost forty-nine years ago, this man so scantily arrayed in his chair died, and even then, his likeness was far from complete. Today, if I attempt to call up a picture of him in my mind, he takes on the appearance of a character actor in an old movie, in black-and-white and before Technicolor—someone like Sidney Greenstreet or, more suitably, Charles Coburn who, in fact, had been a friend and bar chum at the Players Club and even helped produce one of my father's historically thickened plays.

I visualize this father character making entrances and exits in his rooms at the Chelsea, lighting and relighting his pipe, hunched over his desk covered with papers and manuscripts there or in a farmhouse rented for the summer. I would be brought east from Kansas City to perform in both these settings, almost like an extra for a scene and, later when he became confined to a chair like Lionel Barrymore, it was I who appeared and disappeared during leaves from the navy or during university breaks. So, our turns together on the same stage were brief, certainly improvised and for reasons I've already tried to understand in *Last Stands: Notes from Memory.*

The person who had dressed me so formally for this picture was undoubtedly my mother. The original photograph appeared in an article in a New York newspaper—a feature on the aging poet and his young family doing the city sights. Together. My mother's image does not appear in the piece, though the photographer must have wanted to take her picture as well. Raven-haired and vibrant of expression, she was an extraordinarily good-looking woman and, at thirty-six, her beauty had reached its zenith. But she preferred to stay behind the scenes, as she often said, though she had usually stage-managed the scenes, these photo opportunities as we say these days, as if to prove to the world that we were a family. Her Irish pride would permit nothing less, but I've come to suspect her shyness was calculated to stimulate an attention she professed to abhor. After all, she had been of the theatre.

But my inquiry this morning, this washed-out likeness of my father and me on the table beside my portable typewriter, has to do with that "search for the father" as Stanley Kunitz puts it; that ancient quest all poets seem to talk about from Homer on down. In my case, I have both much and little to go on. The facts of his life (not always accurate but who am I to argue) are available in numerous reference tomes, in critical essays and monographs and in a biography now being written. The poundage of his own written output bend several shelves in my library, and his diaries are packed in a safety deposit box. Letters and journals and unfinished manuscripts spill from two steamer trunks in storage while a much more extensive collection can be accessed in the University of Texas Library. A lot of him is all down, on every page and in every footnote, but these documents that give scholars a familiar acquaintanceship are useless to me.

Nor can I piece out his person from those accounts recited by my mother over the years, because her narratives have been shaped and reshaped around a will to consecrate their union, to ascribe to it a nature it never possessed, while hiding—either out of loyalty or pride—her own wounds in the light of his genius. When young, my questioning of her was too timid, and now dementia has reduced her likeness of him even more than this fax before me. In fact, he has completely vanished from the screen of her memory.

So, what I am left with is second-hand, abbreviated and possibly just a paste-up at that, while what is missing is the sensual aura of the man; the smell and feel of him, the handling and warmth of him on a cold morning, the rub and texture of his ordinary stubble. All children, but especially boys, I think, need to come of age within the embrace of an adult male or else they might seek that domain in strangers later. Or sometimes, turn that search into metaphor. The relationship of father and son has its own sensuality, its own special eroticism which requires satisfaction and which, happily, in my case, was supplied by the hard, immigrant's mentorship of my maternal grandfather, Tom Coyne. Yet, a scrap of that hunger has compelled me to attach myself to older role models, no doubt to their alarm; senior writers such as Kunitz whose poetry so movingly weighs this same loss. His father committed suicide before he was born.

So the pangs are reawakened from time to time, as this old photograph has done this morning. The date cannot be discounted. My birthday. As Montaigne has taught us, the only record we can truly verify is our own, so perhaps I carry within my personal album a picture of my father that is far more complete than what I have sought fruitlessly elsewhere. My children are now distant from me geographically as they say I was to them, even as I passed through the rooms of their childhood, and perhaps now they can only visualize a faint transparency of the solid figure I thought I was. They have the advantage of miles of home movies and family snapshots, but these are mostly of them and allow only a fleeting glimpse of this wily shadow, their father. After all, I was the photographer, so I'm absent from these pictures with a couple exceptions—striding down our driveway in Hyde Park, New York, or at the wheel of our little sloop off the coast of New England. Another bit of stage-managing like my mother's? The motivation may have been the same; to preserve a history of children and their mother;

a midcentury, middle-class American family going about its daily minutiae, but without the father. Even that John Wayne imitation strolling down the driveway was rigged—I had set the camera on a tripod and filmed myself automatically.

Surely, they were as stung by my absence as my father perplexed me. I excluded them from my attention and imagination in the same way my father kept me from his hotel suite, exiled me to Kansas City. It is Christmas Eve, and I am almost fifteen. My mother has sent me up to his rooms as she waits downstairs in the hotel lobby. They have been living apart for several years. I am on Christmas break from boarding school, and my mother has determined that this scene be played out, part of the tragedy she keeps running in her head. Something from Euripides perhaps. My father speaks to me through the partly opened door. His face is peculiarly sectioned. I cannot come in. I cannot stay with him, this night. He celebrates with others. So, I return with my mother to her meager corner of an apartment shared behind a bookstore on East End Avenue, my chagrin hardening into a resolve never to make such a foolish errand for love again. Similarly, my children must have looked vainly for me as I peered at them through the viewfinder.

Where is Poppa, they must have asked each other, though I was in the room with them, sitting in the library of the old farmhouse we shared in Columbia County. My attention was elsewhere, just outside the picture. Why is Poppa mad? No doubt my anger was felt, spilling over to scald them or their mother with a look, a silence. Honesty about the past, to paraphrase St. Augustine, may be about all we can hope to achieve in the present; therefore, let me admit belatedly that this rage was against myself. I had only been looking for a clean, well-lighted place in which to work and had somehow walked into this bourgeois cell that seemed to stifle me.

The children of my father's first marriage must have felt a similar numbing chill that hissed from the weld he had attempted to make of his two selves. On one side, the successful lawyer who appeared briefly in their rooms to kiss them goodnight, a respectable Chicago burgher who then sat down to dinner served by maid and butler. While behind that silent screen projection ran the wild unedited footage of a prairie wannabe. He saw himself as Apollo forced into a three-piece suit, and he knew that he had gone to the tailor on his own. Oh, I can savor the delicious depth of that self-pity and feel the scourge of it biting him!

One daughter would never forgive him this deception. Another would spend her life pursuing the same muse in the hope of encountering him someplace in that wood. His son, my half-brother, responded to the betrayal with ire made indelible; permanently souring him. Yet, his filial need was so strong, as if sickened on the very food it desired, that he could never blame his father but lay about with broad swipes, even to include my mother falsely for breaking up that genteel household. But, I digress.

Those three children and I grew up strangers to one another, though bonded by the sightings we made of the same apparition. Later, my own children were to join this frightened circle. All of us can tell each other the same ghost stories, for the specter that haunts me, that vaguely manifests itself on this fax on my desk, is of the same species that walked away from them and down the driveway. Out of the picture. One abuser breeds the next—we know that now whether it be individuals or peoples, and so it must be with fathers. The taste for a father denied makes for an appetite never fully satisfied in others, in work or ambition. No amount of picture making or posturing can assuage the sensual hunger.

My own hunger sometimes seeks its fill in dreams, not an uncommon phenomenon. Some years ago, the aroma of my father's pipe drew me half-awake. The familiar smell of the Prince Albert tobacco he favored circled and hung in my semi-consciousness, and, without opening my eyes, I knew he was standing at the foot of the bed, contentedly puffing and observing me sleep. I could visualize him, no need to open my eyes, though he had been gone from this world many years. He watched over me and seemed pleased by how I had turned out, and I snuggled down beneath this watchful love, like a child and comforted by his sentry. The blessing I had sought from him in life, he gave me in a dream.

So, on this birthday, I make this wish; that I crawl back into my father's arms to feel his abrasive, unshaven cheek on mine, and then that I reach down and gather up my own children and hold their sibling sweetnesses tight, giggling and skewing on my lap. We will be like one of those antique monumentals of togetherness, generations scrambling over each other. Perhaps, this old anchorage outside my window brings such antiquities to mind. The ancient Greeks dropped anchor here to trade and plant their olive trees while telling stories to each other of errant fathers.

1996

Leaving the Party

Here's a journal note for March 6, 1994. I am in Woodstock, Vermont, visiting my son who is in school nearby. I am waiting for him and his girlfriend in the bar of the Woodstock Inn, and we are to have dinner together. I am having a martini as I write in this journal; the western sky outside grows dark. "A last band of pewter behind the bare limbs of trees. It is still very much winter. Outside."

Inside, the mellow ambiance of this snug taproom (pewter here too on plate rails and behind the bar) combines with an excellent martini to stir a sense of well-being. The day's skiing has been very good; the snow especially fine and the weather bright. I am to take an early morning plane back to Pittsburgh, warmed by my son's success and his newly discovered self-confidence. In Pittsburgh, Kathleen waits to take me in her arms. A balmy gust rises within me, and I become a little lightheaded. My mother may be dying.

Earlier, my wife had phoned me. The retirement home had called to say my mother was not "responding," and that her sugar was dangerously low. She had put down particular provisions for her care; among them, "no skin broken, no invasion of the body." Over the bar piano's discrete tinkling, I can hear her demanding voice set forth these orders in much the same manner, she used to pronounce the rules of grammar and syntax. By the time I reach her doctor, the emergency is over; she has been given extra sugar. It has been a freak accident, the doctor tells me. Something that sometimes happens to a person of her advanced age. She is ninety-five.

"So," my journal asks, "is this long journey coming to an end at last?"

Reading over the entry this morning, I contemplate the dimension those last two words measured within me. At last. I can yet taste the sense of compliance with destiny, an understanding of the gods' will, as I wrote them in my journal. An almost Olympian fatalism suffused me, enhanced by the chilled vodka no doubt; a hubris surely condemned by whatever gods who may have been listening at that moment. At last. A worrisome phrase—ambiguous and sentimental, carrying the suggestion that patience had almost been worn out. So, in that comfortable retreat by an open fire, I raise the martini and make one more note to clarify meaning. "Free at last?"

But not just yet. How prescient of me to put a question mark at the thought. My mother still lives, her body viable and unbreached, her skin unbroken. Some cog within her has lost its mesh with time, but that was always true of her. She was the last to leave a party—her glee in company, her pleasure with the company that provided her an audience, usually overcame the exhausted tolerance of her own company. But more than having a good time kept her lagging at the door.

A lonely childhood, the convent-like solitude of her later life, all created a hunger for good times and sometimes rushed her into relationships she would regret. This determination to outlast everyone at a party—even her hosts—appeared to be a curious competition; one for which she had made up the rules so only she could win. And she was prepared to win at all costs, but on this winter's early evening in Vermont, it looked as if she was giving up the race. I had won.

The Greeks, who apparently found pleasure in all our modern neuroses, dramatized and made strong poetry of parent-child rivalries that often ended in mayhem and slaughter. They seemed to accept these conflicts—even their bloody solutions—as normal for the human being, perhaps as punishments for competing with the gods, and my mother followed their example for she identified with all things Greek. She relished the Spartan origin of her name, Ellen. Euripides and company were among her favorite authors. She lived and taught in Greece at the end of her career, and taught herself the language. Moreover, "The Irish are very Greek," she would proclaim. "The Celts, you know," she would add, leaving her audience open-mouthed and tantalized by the insight.

But is it only Greek? The real and imagined dossier of human experience is stuffed with samplings, from all parts of the globe, of parents and children doing each other in. The morning paper reports such an incident in my own neighborhood of Pittsburgh. Sons gunning down fathers, actually or metaphorically. Fathers disinheriting daughters. Mothers and daughters vying for the same man's attention, usually the husband-father. Mothers and sons.

The American actress Spring Byington made her career out of playing sweet, slightly addled but covertly sharp mothers in countless films, but she was only one interpretation of this species to rise from the Hollywood Oedipiad; let's not forget Fay Bainter and Aline McMahon, before she was blacklisted. My encounters with these amazing "mothers" at the Chief

Theatre on Saturday afternoons made me sick with yearning the rest of the week. They were like nothing I knew, but were embodiments of tenderness—open-armed, quietly tolerant and with a silent wisdom brimming their eyes. The audible is here emphasized, because my mother's voice marshaled any conversation, large or small, with a cutting edge and timbre that could penetrate the densest exchange. If her voice conveyed wisdom it was with an armed escort, the guidons of her handsome, slightly prominent teeth flashing in the avant garde of the proclamation.

"A semi-colon, not a comma, must replace the conjunction omitted in a compound sentence," she would declare over my shoulder. I sit at the dining room table in my grandmother's house, my grammar workbook open, its pages smudged by many erasures. "There! There!" her voice stabs my ear as a stiletto nailed finger impales the linguistic fracture exposed before my dumb blindness. These instructions seemed cruel and unusual punishment to me, because they were extra to the time I put in at Scarritt School. It was unfair that I received the benefit of my mother's graduate studies with Thorndike at Columbia University. Fay Holden never raked over Mickey Rooney's grammar in the Andy Hardy films. I bet, even today, he doesn't know what a comma splice is and is probably a whole lot happier for it. But I had to excel, to be at the top of the fifth grade. In sharing her pedagogical techniques, she thought she was being helpful, and she wanted me to win the test. For her sake.

Early on, I recognized this competitiveness made her a whole lot different from Andy Hardy's mother, and my resentment of this difference caused a selective deafness to her voice that, over the years, gradually dulled the central nerve of affection. Filial love never took root; I just didn't like her. I expect, in her mind, the intensity if not ferocity of these tutoring sessions was justified by the brevity of her infrequent visits back to Kansas City to see me and check on my education; my care in her parents' home. Scraping time from her own work in New York to observe these maternal duties drove her to use the time constructively. No time for fooling around. No hugging or kissing. My curious abandonment, with all its references in different lore and legend (oh, how I identified with those characters as I came on them in the library) went on for fourteen years until my grandparents became too infirm to run a household. "Come and get your kid is what your grandfather said to me," she often told me as if to enlist my allegiance against her father for breaking up this happy arrangement.

Not just schoolmates and a neighborhood, a familiar city, I also left a province of affection gently maintained by two people whose love and support of me asked nothing in return; no workbooks to erase and erase until the blanks were filled in correctly. This halcyon clime was suddenly exchanged for an intemperate zone where my every response was tested for accuracy, and where wrong answers were quick marched to a public scaffold. It finally occurred to me that the competition was with her, not with schoolmates. My mother was my adversary, and she wanted to be right, to prove her correctness at my dumb expense. If I should voice a careless, unknowing opinion in company, she would rush to correct me, her voice rising with ridicule, as if to distinguish herself from my ignorance while, at the same time, beating others to the punch, so to speak. Recently, I have come across her own report cards from grade school and high school, and she received mediocre grades. What am I to make of that?

Now it is odd that the same nurturing couple who raised me in Kansas City were probably responsible for this fierce competitive nature that confronted me. As a child, my mother's keen intellect received no encouragement— quite the contrary. My grandfather's peripatetic search for his proper citizenry had moved them from Kansas City to a sheep ranch in the Ozarks to the Panama Canal—then under construction and for which he ran a railroad—and then back to the Ozarks, so by the time she was nine years old, little Fay Fay, as she called herself, had yet to go to school. With the help of a hired girl on the farm, she had taught herself to read, but mathematics instruction was beyond the help. Odd too that my grandmother, who had wanted to be a teacher, made no effort to put her daughter into a school, hire a tutor even. Was it because as a young woman she had had to drop out of teachers college and go to work to support her father who had lost everything in foolish land speculation? Perhaps, in her mind, this bitter experience made education for women a vain exercise. Why try if the traditional, homely duties allotted to the gender trumped the desire for enlightenment? Why give her own daughter the same false hope that had broken her heart and would eventually lead her into the passive depression that ruled the rest of her life?

My grandfather in his attack on the world, his charge toward the lines drawn up against his full citizenship, probably had no time to consider his daughter's education. Maybe he delegated this assignment, in some kind of military post chain of command, to his wife. Whatever the reasons, neither seemed very concerned about this pretty little girl who laboriously read tales from the Grimm Brothers to the cook by the light of a kerosene lamp until, as family legend has it, she threw a fit in the living room of that Ozark farmhouse. She told them they would have to put her into school. They would find a school for her. And they would do it right now. She was nine

years old, and her personality had come on a voice and the imperial nature
that would make people stop and listen. So, they moved back to Kansas
City and the better schools. She went on to the University of Chicago and
then Columbia University. "There she goes," my grandfather would say in
a half-amused, astounded response to something she did or said. He would
clear his throat as if he were speaking through the dust raised by her passage.

But the freedom won by her intellect was brief. She married a man who
had spent most of his life in the nineteenth century, whose instincts and
attitude toward women were shaped by that century's prejudices and beliefs.
Born in 1868, my father had enjoyed close friendships with remarkably
creative women such as Tennessee Mitchell, Lillian Gish, and Edna St.
Vincent Millay; yet, he ultimately had difficulty reconciling the value of a
woman's mind with a woman's body, and the ecstasies to be found in both
raised exasperating conflicts in him. There is a certain kind of man, usually
of high intellect or an ideologue of some stripe, who is drawn to and seeks
out intelligent women—it is part of his erotic kit—but after winning the
woman's affection, he will attempt to remake or subvert her mind and
even dismiss its contributions. These men keep a seraglio in the back of
their heads where all women, however intelligent, are to be quartered. In
my mother, my father had inspired the idolization of a young and beautiful
bed-mate with an excellent mind that had been disciplined and shaped by a
formal education far superior to his. Moreover, she had the will to use what
she had learned. In all probability, he must have felt threatened between
orgasms and his response was to try to put a halter over her head. For her, it
must have seemed like her childhood all over again and perhaps a scene such
as took place in that Ozark living room twenty years before, was reenacted
in those rooms on the second floor of the Chelsea Hotel.

To imprison a freedom simultaneously conceives its liberation, and my
mother's response was to set up a separate "study" where she could pursue
her books; specifically, her thesis on Philip Freneau, the so-called poet of
the American Revolution. It was a self-imposed exile where her intellectual
achievements were to be recognized, and, come to think of it, not all that
different from her father's flight into the Yucatan to seek the recognition of
his talents refused him in the United States. I think my parents' relationship
became a contest as to who had the floor. Content to sit at his feet for a
time, she could still taste the delicious freedom she had briefly enjoyed,
hearing the echo of her own voice calling herself to come out and play
with ideas. The gay independence of her flapper interlude, as qualified as

that independence may have been, seemed betrayed in this old poet's sour domain. She was built to excel, to win; she was, after all, her father's daughter. So, the volume of her voice, argumentative, hearty, enthusiastic, demanding, inventive, expanded until the suite at the Hotel Chelsea could no longer contain it. The sound drowned out all other voices, even mine.

Eventually, she would have the podium to herself, an empty forum over which she stood guard. As the widow of the poet, she achieved an authority that none of her studies had gained her—inside information, if you will, that no one else could out-talk. She outlasted the company, had won over all challengers by simply outliving them. But it was an ironical finish for she had the field to herself—a sad if not qualified victory as all those by attrition are. But, the desire to compete remained; yet, it takes at least two to make a contest. There I was.

I've often wondered why, with her own history, she enrolled me in mediocre schools once I left Kansas City. They were "good enough," she often said, and maybe they were; so I hesitate ascribing any other motive other than the excuse she gave—that she was too busy keeping my failing father upright to spend time and energy placing me in better places. On the other hand, she worked hard to get a friend's son accepted by Fordham Prep, but she did so, she said, because the friend paid her for her efforts. So, the suspicion nags me that she might have been rigging the race from the beginning. Later, this thought would be darkened by her response to my family biography. Initially, she refused to grant me permission to use letters and poems of my father's over which she held the copyright and which were essential to the book's integrity and purpose. She relented grudgingly only after my wife shamed her into doing so, but then waited for the imprimaturs of the *New York Times Book Review, Time, Newsweek,* the *New Yorker,* and other authorities before signing on her appreciation of the book.

So, is this long journey—or better to say *race*—coming to an end, at last? Her body has become a sack for its bones, and her mind washed away by dementia. The once bold and beautiful Irish countenance has withered to resemble the mummified visage of Rameses II. But she is yet not silent. At times, her eyes gleam with the sport to attack a premise, to skewer a foolish thought, but the sound that issues from the mouth is the yap yapping of a simian creature. The old impulse to control the narrative, eloquent and wittily seasoned, remains like a dumb reflex that is unable to affect closure and must run itself down. The means to articulate the parts of the speech, the context and syntax, have been blown away. Her eyes above the yammer look out desperately as if part of her knows she makes nonsense but can do nothing about it. They fix upon me with an eerie light perhaps to transmit the meaning of the babble by the force of their concentration.

But sometimes, I find her look measuring me, estimating my strength and endurance. Or is this only in my imagination, conditioned as I have become to the contest between us? With the proper nutrients regularly poured in one end, this feeding tube she has become can almost indefinitely function. Recently, the nursing home has begun to use a "waist restraint" on her at night. It is for her safety they tell me, because she has slipped off her bed a couple of times—her very weightlessness has become a hazard. Strapped down, restrained; the irony is lacking for the race goes on. I see it in her eyes—to finish first is to finish last.

1996

Everyone Was Alive in 1924

I am standing at a urinal in the men's room of the City Theater in Pittsburgh, Pennsylvania; it is intermission. We have come to see a new play about Andy Warhol—a local boy whose family's business was scrap metal and whose own destiny was to collect and catalog the waste products of our century.

I observe the protocol of the urinal, neither looking to the left or right, nor down, but straight ahead at the wall only a few inches from my eyes. Often, the time spent attending this basic need is enlivened by scribbled graffiti; compact personal histories, an urgent telephone number or sometimes a cartoon for the illiterate, so one's time is not entirely poured down the drain. However, on this night in this men's room, a small neatly printed broadside of poetry is offered my contemplation.

> Midway in our life's journey, I find myself
> In dark woods, the right road lost. To tell
> About the woods is hard, so tangled and rough
> And savage and thinking of it now, I feel
> The old fear stirring: death is hardly more bitter.

Certainly not the suave rendering of the *terza rima* employed by Robert Pinsky, but the words were unmistakably Dante's. As my bladder drains, I am reading the opening lines of "The Inferno." The next day, and after several phone calls, I learn this poster is part of a campaign mounted by the Allegheny County Health Department to urge people to wash their hands after using the facilities. Similar posters with a variety of quotations, both poetry and prose and by different authors, have been fixed above urinals and toilet bowls throughout the county. My informant at the health department proudly tells me that not only such classic authors as Dante have been enlisted in this *cause de sanitaire,* but also contemporary writers have granted permission to use excerpts from their writings. "We have Judy Blume also," he says.

So, Blume and Dante, an unlikely team to spur good toilet habits, though Judy may have more to say on the subject than Alighieri. But, curiously, the great master's eloquent surmise of his century's end is not accompanied by any plebeian admonition about using soap and water. Apparently, the Allegheny County Health Department has confidence in the public's imagination—our ability to find new meaning in these ancient lines—that halfway through life and lost in the dark wood of our own century, we damn well better wash our hands.

A lot of us, clean hands or not, are midway through our journey; the millennium is upon us and some predictions make the wood very dark indeed. Morning papers report computerized schemas of asteroids striking the earth to create massive tidal waves, the height of the Empire State Building, that will demolish coastal cities around the globe. Unstoppable strains of virus wait patiently for the right Tuesday or Thursday to decimate the human population. The weather is getting terrible. Surely our civilization has become rough and tangled as we totter to the end of the century, of the millennium, reaching for any hook on which to hang hope. Butter is—after all—better and pills have been formulated that will restore memory, hairlines, and flagging erections.

"Everyone was alive in 1924," my mother used to boast at parties. Born in 1899, she was a child of the century and boosted the date of 1924, as a kind of watershed, over the heads of younger contemporaries—those who had had the bad luck to be born later in the century than 1924. Like Andy Warhol and me. It was one of the marked cards she dealt out in the competitive game she made of personal relationships; a way to best her audience by implying their birth dates were on the wrong end of the calendar. All of us in the room felt a little cheated, and though we might be aware that we really weren't responsible for our birth dates, we knew we had missed out! We wanted to be part of this marvelous company in this brilliant century.

Oddly, her boast had some truth to it. If not *everyone,* most of the people who put their mark on the twentieth century were alive or had been born by that date—world leaders, scientists, military heroes, writers, and artists—they were all around. Look them up. But to recite the deeds of this class of 1924 is to recall the horrors of this century also and to raise a dirge so commonplace that it has all the freshness of a toothpaste jingle. Their greatest achievement has been in the efficient and systematic slaughter of fellow humans. The Somme, Auschwitz, Hiroshima, Bosnia—it's not a complete list. Avarice governs the professions and the academy, and cupidity is written into the bottom line of every industry whether it rolls cigarettes or prints books. Men and women find little to like in each other. The overall picture is an Inferno of our own making; though, modernists that we are, we insist on piecing out our century's identity with a Switzer or an Auden here; a Curé or a Matisse there when actually, as Andy Warhol single-mindedly demonstrated, our civilization has become a technically proficient but redundant pornography.

In all probability, human beings are a rogue species and only put in control of the planet by the chance rock or two that knocked out the giant lizards who preceded us. My friend, Jeffrey Schwartz, the paleontologist, corrects this simplistic view, saying that all species seem to have a date of expiration stamped into them, and the dinosaurs would have probably disappeared on their own. But that's for another digression. Whatever, the superior intelligence that has swelled our frontal lobes has not engendered a corresponding wisdom, and if there are gods to witness this fatuous sit-com, they must have turned off long ago. Is there any wonder that some resist the wizardry of cloning new humans from old—must we go through all of this mess again to reencounter our history in some Borgesian mirror that will guarantee our extermination?

Justice, that supreme vanity of the human ego, has become the principal synthetic of our century. In America, in Pittsburgh, justice has been subverted by a history we cannot seem to leave behind, that we seem doomed to reinvent and repeat. Our most grievous fault as a society was supposedly addressed 133 years ago only to become our dominant hypocrisy today. Much of our population, our citizenry, yet lives in a spiritual and economic slavery. Racism is alive and we are unwell. Welfare is little more than a reprise of the old plantation songbook—roof and board in lieu of freedom—of acceptance. Surely, African Americans are a patient lot; surely, they are not the docile creatures of the cruel stereotypes. Or, are they only citizens who obey the law?

Martin Luther King Jr. was born in 1929, so he was not one of the "every ones" and that may explain why his mark on the century may be mainly due to his manner of leaving it. Meanwhile, his image has been appropriated to promote many careers and goals, few of which have anything to do with the reason he marched on Selma. He appears on T-shirts and postage stamps along with Marilyn and Elvis who, incidentally, didn't make the cut either. Questions yet remain about his assassination, and ambiguity surrounds the assassin and rightfully so because we are all guilty of the crime. Whoever pulled the trigger in Memphis did so on behalf of the American Twentieth Century.

Here in Pittsburgh, such criminal determinations are just as murky. A couple of years ago, a black motorist was stopped for a minor traffic violation by several white suburban policemen. About twenty minutes later, he lay dead from the application of police batons, their knees and feet. Certainly, the lowest-powered equity meter must register something wrong about this event? Let's say he may have complained about the police stopping him, even resisted arrest, but are our police so unskilled, so poorly trained, that several of them cannot restrain an unarmed "perpetrator" this side of killing him? Did Johnny Gammage during that early hour of morning that was to be his last become the "smart-mouthed nigger" all of us deep down in our white beings want to see punished? So, in the last analysis, maybe the police were only doing their duty and, so far, two juries seem to support this premise by being unable to agree that some kind of crime was committed. Recently, the federal government has refused to intervene. We carry this shoddy account of the right road lost into the new century, the next millennium. Can our future be any more bitter?

Dante was banished from his beloved Florence in 1302, leaving the city limits behind forever along with the century in which he spent most of his life. No wonder he consigned so many of his contemporaries to the circular dungeons of his imagined hell. His life was encompassed by a savage civil war of fifty years' duration, during which he witnessed honor and justice debauched in every corridor and chamber, even in the Papal See where influence with Jesus could be bought—talk about special interests and lobbyists! Those miraculous cathedrals are stone metaphors for the intricate treacheries and hypocrisies of the period. But then there was Beatrice. Her virtuous innocence was to inspire him for a lifetime; it's all he had but it was clearly enough. On the other hand, he only had one glimpse of the girl when she was just nine years of age, so who knows what differences a year or two would have made.

By the time she died at ninety-eight years, almost running down the century, my mother had outlived most of the people who had made the history of these last one hundred years. No doubt, she may have felt she had scored a final point in the continual competition that was her life. They were an anointed alumni, a class of which she was proud to be a part, but I sometimes wonder if, toward the end, she ever felt a bit cheated herself; that she had competed so hard to be part of that class of 1924. I for one—and with the approval of the Allegheny County Health Department—will flush them down the drain and wash my hands of them.

1997

Brother Story

I have three friends who are as close as brothers—certainly as close as I will ever get to having brothers. One is a businessman, the second a painter, and the third, a journalist-screenwriter. They do not know each other, and we seldom see each other; only occasionally talk on the telephone. Yet, I know that should destiny throw me a curve, they would be at my side. And, in fact, this has happened a couple of times.

Over the years, we have become a singular audience of the human follies, and though this special perspective has joined us, we do not have that unique bond produced from sharing that common adversary—the same father. It seems to me that brothers, no matter their differences, are born with a peculiar survival instinct, a common urge to defend against their father.

I shared the same father with Hardin Wallace Masters, though some thirty years separated us, and this temporal distance was even further marked off by the divorce that sundered his family life, as it was to make mine possible. Such as it was. Our estrangement began almost at the moment of my birth and—to confound the poor man even more—to a woman the same age as he. The distance between us was too great for either to hail the other and he carried the distinction to the grave—even to chisel the gap on his tombstone. "The elder son."

Half-brother. The appellation suggests something missing, and it is a void I have attempted to fill, to reach out across my thoughts to my sibling; even, once or twice, affect a reconciliation within the illusion of my fiction. And now, these pages. But he became a ceaseless competitor for our father's approval, and, sadly—and by his own admission—even schemed to deny me my small inheritance from this single progenitor destiny had determined for us to share. It is the puny stuff that an Aeschylus or a Shakespeare made into great art but which remains a bourgeois melodrama in our hands.

Family records tell me little about him beyond the bare facts. He briefly attended Exeter Academy and never finished college. He tried working as a stockbroker but the 1929 crash blunted that career; then, he found success in banking and insurance. He married a pleasant woman, but they had no children; complications that followed a miscarriage denied him offspring.

He served in the navy during World War I and ended up a lieutenant colonel in the Army Air Corps in the Second War though not as a flyer but in that service's supply division.

In fact, the first time I was to meet him, he was wearing this uniform, a captain's silver bars on his burly shoulders. I was dazzled. At sixteen, I had discovered a brother who was an officer in the Army Air Corps, but to my confusion, my father was not impressed.

"The runt is showing up," he told my mother one afternoon in the lobby of the Selwyn Hotel in Charlotte, N.C. He waved Hardin's letter as she returned from the Country Day School where she had been hired to put together an English department.

Thanks to her, the three of us were just emerging from hard times. At seventy-six, my father was recovering from a period of illness and self-neglect, a spiritual and physical impoverishment that had separated him from us and most of his friends and from which, almost single-handedly, my mother had pulled him. He had been near death in every sense.

This was 1944, and we were on the road, living in hotels and supported by my mother's teaching jobs. Though my father was about to receive a substantial prize for his life's work, that work in poetry was long behind him, and he would look back on that work and that life as he sat in hotel lobbies among potted palms, to make ongoing surveys as sour and as worn as the brass spittoon that was often at his feet. The war was on, and I was resentfully attending a small college nearby, because I wanted to get into the battle—preferably as a flyer—but I was too young.

So, to my astonishment, here I have a brother who was "in the war" and if not as a flyer in the Army Air Corps, he no doubt knew flyers, probably rubbed shoulders with a few of them, so I took my brother's side even before I met him, closing ranks, as it were, against our sire's dismissal of him. How could our father not be proud of this son? "He doles out socks," my father said out of the corner of his mouth. We were having our dinner in the hotel's cafeteria. I was home for the weekend from college.

It would be some years before I caught on to the old poet's guile that skillfully manipulated his two families, played one off against the other. This evening, over the rice pudding, he tells my mother and me of Hardin's navy episode in World War I—twenty-six years back! It is an old story for her.

"They would have sent him to prison. Maybe shot him," he adds gravely. "Absent without leave in wartime is considered desertion, a capital offense."

"Oh really," my mother says lightly and puts a match to a cigarette. She has only recently taken up smoking; magazine ads said it was good for the nerves. "Shot at sunrise, you mean?"

"I got him off," he continues steely eyed. "I got a judge I knew. Got statements from a doctor that Hardin had pneumonia, was stuck at home." He's being discreet—he had been a lawyer before *Spoon River* after all—and he says no more. But the subtext carries on; he had imperiled his integrity as an officer of the court, had perjured himself to protect this wayward son. Oh well, my mother clanks the several bracelets that always encircled her wrists, we would make the best of the visit.

So, one morning, Hardin and his wife join us for a late breakfast in a cramped booth of the New York Cafe, a greasy spoon across from the hotel where my father appreciated the cook's way with corned beef hash. Certainly, the place's name appealed to him as well, for he felt exiled from New York City here in North Carolina. Hardin had just been assigned to a new post near the state capital of Raleigh, and he looked splendid in his olive-green tunic and officer pinks. He even sported a couple of ribbons on his breast to indicate he had done something well. He had a kind of swagger to him, and the trim moustache seemed to go with his commission. Disappointingly, he is on the short side, but—coming to his defense—I consider our father was no giant either. I am already taller than both of them.

It is a tense encounter at the New York Cafe. Much of the conversation has escaped my memory, but the tone my father took has not. Curt and indifferent; I have never seen him so cold or ungenerous. I feel sorry for Hardin and am angered for him. Later, I was to hear that my father's behavior with Hardin would be quite different during those other family outings; a sunny companionship with him and his sisters. He would become warm and mischievous—the father that I knew. So, this forbidding performance over a poached egg in the crater of corned beef hash was for our benefit, for me and my mother, as if were he to show a scrap of affection for Hardin in our presence would somehow be disloyal to us, the second family. Sadly, he had no real allegiance to any of us, but shared his disaffection equally.

I have become aware that Hardin almost totally ignores my mother, later to take his leave of her in the hotel lobby with a cool correctness. As I said, they were the same age, and this circumstance must have been awkward for her as well—it was their first meeting—she handled it off-handedly with her usual spirited humor. However, the thirty-two-year age difference between her and my father apparently stung Hardin's Methodist rigor with a bite he could not assuage, for my mother's youth served as a handy explanation for his own mother's abandonment. I should have picked up this message Hardin delivered, but my hankering for a brother had scrambled my attention.

The divorce that ended that first marriage had been painful and messy; its sordid details were splashed across the front pages of Chicago newspapers. When my mother and father were married four years later, she became the designated home wrecker, though she had been nowhere near the scene of the accident. Two years later, when I was born, members of that first family swaddled me in the clothes of the ill-gotten offspring like the bastard son in an old romance. Hardin, and in all probability his mother, chose to ignore the true villain of this melodrama, while the lie of my mother's role was cultivated and promoted. For all the while, his father—my father—had been an egregious womanizer and a regular patron of brothels when the game on the street became scarce.

In fact, the poet had hoped to marry a wealthy widow—also some years younger than he—and he chased her for several years, even around Europe, but the lady became discouraged by the prolonged divorce proceedings and lost interest in him. If Hardin needed to blame a woman for the loss of his happy home, another illusion, the woman my father called "Pamela" in his autobiography was the one, but my mother was convenient and would do as the subject for this fraudulent revision.

What I have learned from others about my half-brother suggests he could divide up the truth according to the image he wished to project of himself for his own private viewing; a trait, come to think of it, he might have inherited. Let's give this another turn; I'm not entirely innocent of the trick myself. But, in fact, isn't this a human skill? We take reality apart and then reassemble it to make something different, and this Janus vision has produced both Hiroshima and "A Sunday Afternoon on the Island of La Grande Jette."

My friend Nick tells me that he may not write another book, that he will only create film scripts from now on. His eyes have left the page, as it were, and will cast their sharp insights into our social mores upon the screen. This talk saddens me as both a writer and reader of books—I am committed to books. I am not complaining about one more good writer going over to "the other side," but I will miss the intellectual vigor of his investigative reporting; the fine way he has of atomizing a personality or a political event and then putting the parts back together to provide me with a fresh understanding of them. The motion picture, by definition, means a continual advance of narrative; to pause to reflect on an event, dissect its meaning, makes for a dull movie. It's a different medium, as they say, and its difference from books extends to its portability. A book can be carried in a pocket, opened and read anywhere—try taking a movie to a desert island.

My father had been unable to carry away the books of his library from the house he deserted in Chicago in 1922—the divorce settlement barely left him the copyrights to his own books. So now, here in North Carolina, in exile at the Selwyn Hotel, he tries to get back his Goethe, Shelley, Keats, and Byron and all the other volumes that had layered his thinking, that he had stolen from as writers steal, that had furnished the ambiance of his soul and intellect. He brings them up during this breakfast with Hardin at the New York Cafe, and this part of the conversation, I remember.

ELM: I don't understand why you can't get those books back to me.

HARDIN: I don't know where they are, Dad.

ELM: Has your mother sold them?

HARDIN: I don't think so.

ELM: Then where are they? Those books are my property. I want them back. *(Pause to take a last bite of egg and hash. Some yellow yolk dribbles down over whiskered chin. Mother reaches across table to wipe chin with paper napkin. Father's fixed stare on Hardin does not waver.)* I want them back.

He must have made similar demands before, for I know that he continually raised the subject in letters for the next half dozen years, until his death in 1950. He got the same answer as he received that day in Charlotte. My half-brother knew nothing about the library.

But he did know; in fact, he had most of the books in his possession. Twenty-eight years after our father's death, Hardin published a little chapbook entitled *Edgar Lee Masters: A Biographical Sketchbook of a Famous American Author,* and in an appendix he lists the editions of Blake, Twain, Thoreau, Cicero, and the rest. He had had the books all along.

This sketchbook, as he called it, is ostensibly a tribute to ELM, but it's more of a construction of how Hardin saw himself; a wounded, suffering son who emerges as the benevolent first family patriarch, judiciously filling the void left by the absent father. Seasoned, balanced opinions righteously ring through its pages while the lie of my mother's supposed involvement is not so subtly promoted. For good measure, he parades his magnanimous *ascent* to my father's will, which made my mother sole heir to my father's pitiful estate, though the legal possibility (not to mention the moral probity) of a challenge to my father's last will apparently lay outside his conscience. That he had even considered such a venture—if only to then prove his generosity by rejecting the idea—is a measure of the man, I think.

The publication history of this little book is a curious story. The Fairleigh Dickinson University Press published the volume in 1978, one of twenty-seven titles put out by that organization that year that also included such memorable tomes as *Locomotive Designers in the Age of Steam, New Jersey Women, 1770–1970: a Bibliography, Understanding the Traditional Art of Ghana, At the Grass Roots in the Garden State: Reform and Regular Democrats in New Jersey,* and *Mystical Transformation: The Imagery of Liquids in the Work of Mechthild von Magdeburg.* The list also includes an anthology of Finnish writing, *Snow in May,* which I happen to have in my own library. But the list is typical for such a small university press, a member of a consortium that handles distribution and sales, Associated University Presses.

So how did Hardin Masters, neither an alumnus of Fairleigh Dickinson nor a resident of New Jersey—he had just moved to Arizona from Oklahoma—get his book published by this relatively unknown university press in New Jersey? How did this retired bank president even hear of the press and then invite the consideration by its editors of his manuscript? And why, in the final act, did Fairleigh Dickinson publish the book after a very negative reader's report—provided me by a recent editor?

"The sketches are too brief, often sentimental and in some cases, not very well written. The author is an ex-bank president and ex-insurance company president, and is way up there in the Presbyterian Church. He is also active in the Boy Scouts. His father loathed banks, was a violent atheist and sneered at Boy Scouts. So, in a sense, there really was no rapport between the two. It has been said with validity that the one who knows the least about a great writer is his wife. I guess it can be said that another who knows little about a great writer is his son, especially when the son really had little understanding about his celebrated father."

But there was little in print about Edgar Lee Masters aside from his autobiography, the report goes on, so to publish this manuscript might provide an "elephantine footnote" for future scholarship. It may have provided something else, and here I admit that my novelist's eye colors in some of the blanks of my research.

The writer of that reader's report was Charles Agnoff, a poet who taught in the Fairleigh Dickinson English department. Mr. Agnoff had also been the president of the Poetry Society of America, that hoary den of wannabes and verse lovers founded by Amy Lowell in 1903. Hardin had joined the PSA in the 1970s—the organization had never been adverse to extending membership to patrons regardless of their kinship with Apollo—and in 1971 placed its imprimatur on a slight chapbook, a reminiscence which was mostly composed of about twenty poems from *The Spoon River Anthology.* Neither Hardin nor the Poetry Society of America sought permission to use these poems from my mother, who held their copyright, even though she would have granted that permission. She asked me to write Hardin suggesting he make a formal request for their usage, but he never replied. Possibly, he felt the poems were part of his inheritance—something the judge in the 1922 divorce had denied him—but what justification the Poetry Society of America used for their copyright infringement is anybody's guess. Hardin paid for the chapbook's publication.

So, this little volume seems to have been a run-through for the more ambitious sketchbook that Agnoff—then the president of the Poetry Society—paradoxically "recommended" to Fairleigh Dickinson. A sort of partnership, if you will, had been established. It's possible that Hardin may have also contributed to the publication costs of the second book. It is not unusual for such small presses to be utilized for a personal gain rather than the advancement of a literary or intellectual query. In any event, Hardin's malicious innuendoes and falsehoods can be found on the shelves of university and public libraries. He clearly has had his slanderous revenge.

But my inquiry has foundered in the rank marsh of a family squabble when I had hoped to make a balanced inquiry on the nature of brotherhood such as Montaigne might have made. It is curious that the Master never wrote much about brotherhood in his stone tower but fashioned many essays on friendship. And he had many brothers to write about too, including Pierre, killed by a tennis ball and possibly a seducer of Mme. Montaigne—Pierre's gold chain was found in her jewel box after his death! Now that's a relationship Montaigne never tried to assay, and why not? Could my earlier assertion about brothers banding together against the father be wrong?

Last night my friend Hector and I talked on the phone about the recent earthquake that brought down the ceiling of the basilica of St. Francis in Assisi. He is a painter of estimable reputation and finesse, rich in knowledge of Italy and its art treasures so yesterday's damage reports urged me to call him. Like paying my respects, offer my condolences. I have been to that Umbrian hilltop village only once but the magical serenity of the place, the benevolent history of St. Francis that it celebrates, is a palpable ingredient of my ethos. I can call up the brisk May morning some years ago when I stood beneath that vaulted ceiling and looked up at the gorgeous array of inspiration left there by Giotto, Cimabue, and Martini. I am particularly fond of Simone di Martini.

"Oh, well," Hector said. "They've been up there for six hundred years. We've had them for six hundred years." And so we've been lucky to have that much, he is saying—let's be thankful for what we have had and get on with life. It is a shrewd axiom, unsentimental and positive and probably something St. Francis, a merchant's son, might have endorsed. My friend is a wily accomplice to his feelings and does not always show them in plain cloth; yet he has been open about his family relationships and how his brothers hated him when they were growing up.

The three of them made no common defense against their father in the style I want to portray. Quite the contrary. Where did I get this idea—off of some neoclassic print that shows brothers arming themselves, helmeted but otherwise scantily clad and confronting the muscular anger of a bearded patriarch? "I was my father's favorite," Hector tells me. "My brothers hated me for it. One of them even went after me with a knife." But they have become very close, have grown beyond and over that division now and enjoy warm, respectful relationships.

Perhaps if my half-brother and I had been placed more equally on the chronological scale, we might have managed a similar reconciliation. But the years between us were too steep for Hardin to climb, and our father made no effort to level the ground. In fact, the self-serving asides he put to us raised more barriers.

Hardin does give me a one-and-a-half-page chapter in his memoir, and it is titled "Son Hilary." Not *"Brother* Hilary," mind you, so even at that late date, nearly thirty years after our father's death and both of us grown men, the wound of my birth, my existence still hurt him. Moreover, the actuary tables being as they are, the ex-insurance company president must have assumed my existence would exceed his, so maybe it would be a good idea to get his side of the story down first, on the record such as it is, before I had the final word. As I am having.

The few lines that describe me and our sibling relationship are pathetically transparent, revealing his impoverished need of a father's love. He says that I was "a problem" to my parents though he does not specify in what way. After all, I wasn't the one who went AWOL. More striking is a paragraph in which he reports my father's fondness and high expectations for me, surely a little salt the poet sprinkled in the cut. He directly quotes my father, *Watch out for your half-brother, Hilary: he is a fine boy.*

"This comment always gave my heart a twist," Hardin adds, "because he had so often said to me, 'You are a good boy.'" So could there not be two of us, both fine or good boys? Was Hardin so shortchanged of love that he fiercely competed for any scraps of it; imagined a share of it when it wasn't forthcoming? Such starvation must engender an appetite that can never be sated. It is a sad thought, and sadly, but with a brotherly sense of justice, I stand to condemn that father who so coldly twisted the elder son's heart.

Hector's experience must be untypical; we do come to the aid of the other against the father's deprivations, though the succor may be late in coming.

Some years ago, I carelessly put myself in the way of a farm tractor, and the two tons of equipment inexorably rolled over me. It was a close call. A fraction of an inch one way and the large rear wheel of the tractor would have crushed my head. Luckily, I suffered no serious injuries, no broken bones, but the trauma put me in a hospital for several days, and on returning home, I found my friend Arthur waiting. He had left his publishing business and driven several hours to be with me, to see if he could help my wife in any way.

My recollection is still a little groggy about the occasion; he brought a gift but I can't remember what it was. I do remember, will always remember the gift of his friendship that had brought him to my bedside. To sit and talk with me, to tender the good medicine of his brotherly affection. His only brother was run over and killed before their house two years before he was born—he never knew the little boy. But does he ever think about him? Am I only playing at fiction, but would it be possible that my accident reminded him of that other one years before? Was that accident somehow set aside by my mishap, a second chance granted to be the brother denied him before? I keep meaning to ask Arthur if he ever thinks of that young sibling and has he ever missed him as I have missed mine. Someday.

1995

Winfield Townley Scott
The Exile as Mentor

Can it be that the wise and warlike Athene has come to some of us in the guise of a Stegner, or an Ashberry, or a Bellow to help us take "the dreadful leap" as Byron described it? Are these Mentors assigned to some of us by a higher authority to give counsel and sign recommendations or do we, say some of us, apply to a Stegner or an Ashberry as we might apply for a fellowship—rewarding fellowships in several senses of the word.

Those of us who share these encounters with Mentor, share only the apparition, for this particular guide seems to dispense good deeds and good advice evenhandedly, indiscriminately. Some have been gifted with book contracts, a Guggenheim or a MacArthur—perhaps, a marketable review in the *New York Times*, while others have had line breaks improved, novels focused—even spelling corrected.

Winfield Townley Scott did none of this for me; yet, I recognized him as Mentor when I came to his office at the *Providence Journal* one day in 1950. I had come to thank him for the kind compliment he had given the undergraduate literary magazine I was then editing at Brown University. His column "Bookman's Galley" was a regular feature of the Sunday book page which he had edited for nearly twenty years. Is it only in the room of my imagination, rearranged just so for this essay, that I remember thinking the poet seemed out of place? Despite the pipe tobacco smoke that enwreathed him, his tweed jacket and the nattily knotted knit tie, I want to think I sensed the persona of an exile. More important—and this perception *was* to be proved all wrong in the next twenty years—Win Scott seemed to have made a successful accommodation, had brought his persona as an outsider, inside. The error recognized was to be my invaluable gift.

Scott Donaldson's 1972 biography, *Poet in America: Winfield Townley Scott*, describes our first meeting at the newspaper office. "Masters arrived in a filthy, paint-stained camel's hair coat, 'a god-damned angel in rags,' as Win put it." This black overcoat had been my father's, and I had worn it to paint the ceiling and walls of my apartment on Benefit Street to protect my other clothes in a kind of oedipal twist on prudence. Moreover, I wore this paint-splattered garment to classes and around campus to insult the preppy sensibilities of the Brown campus, because in the last couple of years I had realized my mistake in opting for Brown on my GI bill rather than returning to Missouri and the state university there. So, when I walked into Win Scott's office at the *Journal,* I had self-consciously put on the tattered raiment of an outsider, little suspecting he was trying to make a similar change of clothes, but in reverse. We met, I think, at some sort of personal equinox.

Some biographical reference might be relevant. When I entered Brown in 1948, I had done a couple of years in the navy at the end of WW-2 and had worked on a newspaper in Washington for another nine or ten months. An alumnus of the place, a colleague in Navy PubRel, had urged me to apply and, no doubt, had seconded my application. The school's name had roused my curiosity. Brown?

Growing up in Kansas City, at least in my lower-middle-class northeast section of Kansas City, made the Ivy League a foreign territory. Even though my mother was then doing graduate work at Columbia, the schools which meant something to me were those whose football teams I followed on WDAF radio. Purdue, Northwestern, Michigan, and USC. Notre Dame, of course. Yes, Yale supposedly had a running back who made All-American, but U. of Missouri had quarterback Paul Christman, and Harry Ice was no slouch either. But Brown? You've got to be kidding.

As a member of the last "veteran class," I was told to find my lodgings off campus so that the younger, less-worldly freshmen could move into dormitories on campus. Rooms were scarce. This initial exile was okay by me, and I joined a group of men, most of them veterans too, who viewed the careful, buttoned-down atmosphere on campus with a little scorn. Indeed, to pursue poetry or painting or the theatre was almost to express that scorn. We found rooms and apartments in the decrepit frame houses along a pregentrified Benefit Street, cashing in our monthly GI allotment checks at Irish bars and spaghetti joints with enough left over for a beer and wine blast. We raised the standard of Bohemia. We enjoyed our alienation not to mention the interest of Pembrokers who had discovered the decorum practiced under the campus elms too restricted.

As I say, I came to Win Scott's office that winter of 1950–1951 to thank him for his column's kind notice of a recent issue of *Brunonia.* I had turned the lit magazine into a rebellious pamphlet. The poetry and fiction we printed was to cover our attacks on the university's fuddy-dud policies. We ridiculed the rule for compulsory chapel, where attendance was taken as if for a class. We railed at the student newspaper for passing over a qualified African-American—about one of three enrolled in the student body then—for its editorship. We chastised a fraternity for blackballing Jewish pledges. We questioned President Henry Wriston's priorities, putting up new buildings at the expense of faculty salaries; therefore, faculty retention. My thunderous, if not always grammatical prose, must have become annoying because there were a couple of attempts by the administration to shut down the magazine.

So when I entered Win's office that afternoon, I might have been ready to find a mentor, a rebel-kin who could show me how to live as an outsider. Nor was my own determination to be a writer all that set at this point. I spent most of my undergraduate years majoring in International Relations until Columbia lured away most of the department, three distinguished professors, by better salaries.

But Win's poetry had also prepared me to see him as Mentor. Most of us knew his work and had read his first three books; *Biography for Truman* and *Wind the Clock*. Then, later, *To Marry Strangers*. We read him not just because he had graduated from Brown, but his poems seemed to speak to and for us. The persona of Traman was particularly appealing to those of us who considered Providence to be our Dublin and each of us a Stephen D. Scott's figure encountered his limitations and aspirations, his dreams and sexuality on the same dawn-streaked streets of the same old mill town and in the same way we did. We recognized the route taken and the anger and uncertainty with which it was taken. One poem from *Wind the Clock*, published in 1941, especially struck us. I quote the first stanza of "Five for the Grace of Man" and then the fourth.

> See this air, how empty it is of angels
> Over O'Ryan's barroom. The bum thrown out
> Shoulders the sidewalk, pushes it away,
> His hat rolling and baldspot gleaming
> Under the rain and under O'Ryan's lights

. . . And then this fourth stanza.

> How shall I ever come to any good
> And get my works in schoolbooks if I use
> The rude word here and there, but how shall I
> Let you know me if I bequeath you only
> The several photographs, the family letters?

> There is no image of a tired mind
> Tired of its own vanity for fame.
> I turn in the comfort of the midnight rain
> And as much for pleasure as necessity
> Piss in the river beyond O'Ryan's bar.

These lines of Win Scott's would be quoted, sometimes shouted into the night air over Benefit Street. The word *piss* would swell a drunken chorus. We hailed the poet's boldness to use such a word (this some fifteen years before "Howl") while others, on more sober reflection, would remark on his understanding of our dilemma; to be accepted by schoolbook Brown, we had to keep our feelings buttoned up. But then, *then,* the more prescient would point out; the poet had not only gone ahead and used the rude word, but also had committed the rude act as well and in the open air! Into the river!

His integrity and courage, the audacity of the act, seemed to address me exactly. Sadly, this dilemma of public act and private feeling was never to be resolved by him, and I was to witness how it wore him down over the next twenty years.

In eight more books of poetry, several collections of essays, and a memoir, Scott seemed to eulogize spiritual outcasts. His muse was particularly drawn to the rebels who soothed their own angers, often transformed into a tolerable, dignified regret. He wrote of this despair and how it had been discharged into the mainstream of a given time; a feat he would never succeed in doing though he would often try.

Such figures as the queer fabulist H. P. Lovecraft, Emily Dickinson, the old Socialist Joseph M. Caldwell, Dorr of the Rebellion with his name, Henry Beston of Cape Cod, Freydis, the half-sister of Leif Ericson, and even E. A. Robinson and Mark Twain appealed to him as people who had gone against the grain. Win admired them for their different eccentricities, their insubordination, and how they lived out or out-lived their transgressions. John Greenleaf Whittier might have been a paradigm.

Mr. Whittier and Other Poems was published by Macmillan in 1948. Three years earlier he had published *To Marry Strangers,* his fourth book and a turning point for his maturing voice. The book was praised in print, perhaps egregiously, by Horace Gregory, but savagely trashed by Robert Lowell in *The Sewanee Review.* Seven years Win's junior, Lowell was a year away from his own *Lord Weary's Castle* and his first Pulitzer, so whether his attack was intended as a knockout punch to a potential competitor or a clean, unprejudicial judgment is, I think, a fair question.

In any event, *Mr. Whittier* was to bolster Win's reputation with a number of good reviews from poets like Horace Gregory, again, or Selden Rodman in the *New York Times Book Review*. The title poem has, over the years, proved its value and remains one of Scott's most memorable works as it celebrates the author of "Snow-Bound" who died a pariah because of his radical views on labor and his attacks on slavery. Whittier had been vilified from pulpits; harassed in public. Some people who read his books were jailed. Yet, this same man wrote the gentle poem, "Snow-Bound."

Win's poem is composed in the lengthy, almost casually metered line that he would make his own in subsequent work. He reminds us that Whittier " . . . put the names of our places into his poems." Then, he sounds this lament, "It is so much easier to forget than to have been Mr. Whittier." Halfway through, he offers a variation. "It is easier to leave *Snow-Bound* and a dozen other items in or out of/ The school curriculum than it is to have written them. Try it and see." This 1948 volume contains some of Win Scott's strongest work, including "Gert Swasey," "Pvt. John Hogg," and the very lovely "Memorabilia," but it would be another ten years before his poetry would appear in book form again.

Winfield Townley Scott was born to a middle-class family in Newport, Rhode Island, and he lived there for the first ten years of his life. His father worked in *his* father's hardware store. This place and his place in it imprinted a pattern of discontent and ambition on him that would affect him the rest of his life. For, to be middle class in Newport, R.I. in the early years of this century gave one a curious sense of being "disadvantaged," to use his term, because every summer the enormously rich families of America moved into the huge mansions they had built along the sea front. In his 1961 essay collection, *Exiles and Fabrications,* he writes:

> The influence of such a colony upon the middle-class who live beneath it, more or less dependent upon it, has never been properly studied. Newport, at least, has never been written of in that way—the fictions of Henry James and Edith Wharton and lesser lights take other angles. Yet, I know my orientation was that rich people were the salt of the earth; that we lower breeds were fortunate to glimpse them as they flickered along Bellevue Avenue, and blessed to gaze familiarly, Sunday after Sunday drive, at their great castles between the blue hydrangeas and the sea. It took me years to recover from that obeisance and then a few more to readjust to the observation that a rich man is not necessarily a spoiled son of a bitch.

His Yankee family, overwhelmed as they were by their luxurious neighbors, taught Win at an early age the ground rules of the American success story; pointed out its proof to him during every Sunday drive. At the same time, these demonstrations taught him "what it meant to be an artist in a society where commercial values were the prevailing measure," writes Scott Donaldson in his biography. "Unconsciously, unwillingly, Scott shared those values; they were part of his heritage."

So, Win worked hard at winning prizes for his youthful poems to show his family that this frivolous endeavor *could* receive some material reward. He entered Brown University in 1927. He did well enough in English courses to be elected to Phi Beta Kappa despite a C average in the rest of the curriculum. By his sophomore year, he was writing anarchistic (by Brown standards) columns in the student newspaper, mostly against compulsory chapel. He had also been invited to do book reviews for the *Providence Journal Bulletin,* and even to run the book page during the editor's summer vacation.

So when I walk into his newspaper office during my junior year, he has been the book editor for nearly twenty years and has made the *Providence Journal Book Review* into one of the most respected in the country. Rumpled tweed jacket, dark knit tie, a pipe in his mouth and several more lying about a desk strewn with galley proofs, small boxes of wooden matches here and there—and books everywhere—he was the image of a writer, a successful poet. He could lean back in his chair, puff on his pipe, as he talked persuasively of Robert Frost's importance while sometimes glancing at the small calendar on his desk where the pretty winsomeness of a Petty Girl held the luscious nakedness of her breasts in her arms. I think I must have fallen in love.

I will never forget the sound of his voice. It carried forth from a deep, throaty register that could eloquently shift emphasis as if he were sighting a new thought, another angle on the subject, just as it rounded the corner of his consideration. More than one woman, including two women I was to marry, claimed this melodious sound gave them a sexual rush. His voice rose out of his chest with a quality that seemed liquid or even liquored, as some would speculate because of the heavy drinking that was to come, but I think what we heard were echoes from the bottom of a profound resonance. A pool of tears.

On this day, he spoke to me with great kindness and interest. He spoke lightly but no less approvingly of my published arguments with the Brown establishment. He asked whom I was reading. Was I interested in poetry? The question was almost off-hand, asked with the roundish head turned away, the heavy-lidded eyes obliquely inspecting me. My father had died the previous spring, and I was wearing an unearned celebrity, the son of Edgar Lee Masters, with difficulty and not a whole lot of grace. Win changed the subject. What teachers did I enjoy? When I mentioned the Shakespearean scholar William Hastings, he clucked his approval, nodded and hummed. Hastings had been his mentor, had guided him through the English curriculum toward Phi Beta Kappa.

Out of this first meeting, came an invitation to drop by his house on a weekend afternoon where I was to meet his wife and children. Ellie Scott was then about twenty-nine, eleven years younger than he, and only a few years out of Bennington. Their affair while she was still a student, and Win still married, had been hot and dramatic—somewhat scandalous in prim Providence society. For him, the affair had been both a roil of reawakened sexual energy and a moral anguish as well, especially because of the son he had fathered in the first marriage. After a hurtful divorce, Win married Eleanor Metcalf in 1946. I was aware of a building on the Brown campus by that name, but only gradually did I realize that Ellie was a member of one of the wealthiest families in Rhode Island.

But she also was a rebel. She wore her glossy honey-brown hair loose and halfway down her back, and she moved with an athletic ease. She was opinionated and expressed her opinions frankly and clearly with dashes of an infectious wit. The workings of her intelligence seemed to illuminate the features of her face, light up the eyes behind the heavy-framed glasses to give the whole expression an unexpected beauty. She was everything I had heard a Bennington girl was supposed to be—lusty, intellectual, and foul-mouthed. *Fucking* was her favorite participle.

So seeing him in that sunny, large living room on Morris Avenue, a house given them by her father I was to learn later, it seemed to me that Win Scott had won all the chips. Two small children playing about his feet, tended by a young and vibrant wife, this established poet and important book review editor played the genial host to me, mixing drinks and moving casually to the white mantled fireplace, to relight his pipe and continue the amusing digest of a recent chat with Bill Williams—that's William Carlos Williams.

He furnished his remarks and observations with an astounding lexicon of quotations from poems and the classic scholars, from biographies of great men and their great words—from history and science, all easily called up from memory to add charm or depth to the conversation. This facility always amazed me, though that afternoon my ignorance was embarrassed as well; only recently had I discovered that when people spoke of Eliot, they meant T. S. and not George.

With three books of poetry under his belt and some awards coming in, just recently the Shelley Memorial, Win moved with the assurance and quiet authority of a writer who had been "tapped." That year John Ciardi had brought out his anthology *Mid-Century American Poets* which included Win's work along with that of Roethke, Bishop, Jarrell, Schwartz, Rukeyser, Eberhart and, of course, Robert Lowell. " . . . his work is indispensable to the make-up of this book," Williams Carlos Williams wrote of Win's contributions in a review. He was asked to serve on literary panels, to evaluate and give awards to other writers. So, it seemed to me he had made it—his rebellion had won.

And so it must have seemed to him, for within the year, he resigned from the newspaper to devote all his energies to his poetry. He told himself, and others, that he had worked hard for almost twenty years, creating a book review of distinction, while cribbing time and space for his own work, and now it seemed only just—surely, the gods must approve—that he accept the opportunity his marriage to Ellie Metcalf afforded him. Perhaps, this might be a reward from these same gods. Her youth and intelligence had fired up the flames banked down within this forty-year-old Puritan sensibility. Sex and poems had "Come Green Again" to cite one of the poems he wrote to celebrate the dual refreshment. The Metcalf millions could free his muse as it supported his new family; after all, it was inherited wealth and what better way to use it?

A couple of years later, Win and his growing family—a third child and second daughter had been born—left Providence for good; they moved to nearby Hampton, Connecticut, and into a well-proportioned old farm house that Ellie set about remodeling. She added on a large, austerely handsome glass-walled library that also became a family room. She painted the wide-board floors in brilliant greens, yellows, and reds.

But if the gods seemed to approve—Win really did not. He sought endorsements from others for this self-exile from Providence and its workaday world, finding a consensus in others but never within himself. In letters, he sometimes referred to himself as a "kept man." Not even the consent of Wallace Stevens, nearly a god of the time, helped. During a pause in their deliberations on the 1953 Bollingen Committee, Stevens turned to his fellow panelist, Scott, and said, "We have poets in the insurance business and poets teaching college. It's time we had a poet—off in a village in Hampton, Connecticut—who does nothing but think of his life: that is to say, of his poetry."

But, in the early 1950s, Win Scott's life and art seemed to swell with the rising of each sun. In August of 1954, the Scott family left Hampton, during the height of that year's severe hurricane, to follow that sun westward to Santa Fe, New Mexico. It was supposed to be a place of liberation for both him and Ellie—not another exile. But during those first eight years of our friendship, from 1950 to 1958, he was unable to get another book published.

It was during these eight years that he assumed the activity and influence of a mentor that this essay has been attempting to describe. The reader who has worked through the foregoing scramble might understand, by now, that my effort has been to present his role as different from the mentor who guides a younger artist through different channels, from one opportune marker or grant to another and finally into a safe cove of fame.

I shudder to think of some of the stuff I sent him to read during this period. He responded as if all my clumsy fictions were important, deserved the careful readings he gave them. At Ellie's request after his death, I gave all of my letters from Win to the John Hay Library at Brown, so his exact responses are beyond my immediate research. But, here in Pittsburgh, I can review some excerpts from memory. Place and character were always important to him as both writer and reader. He went for straight, uncluttered language and called me down on my effusions pretty regularly. Not often enough, perhaps. He insisted on authentic motivations, the believable decisions a character might make in a narrative. The gratuitous phrase, the unnecessary adjective were often gently shaken from my prose and held up to the light for my understanding.

"I'm not convinced your character would turn that way, considering his background," he might write. Or, one time, that distinctive, speculative voice came slyly over the phone, "Do you think it absolutely necessary to describe her thighs as *silky?*" Then, the professorial manner broke into an ingratiating chortle meant to soothe hurt feelings and to convey a sense of equals—two men who shared a common knowledge—the feel of a woman's thighs. Why bother with the adjective?

His continued, generous reading of my work encouraged me as it corrected my excesses. He introduced me to the work of other writers he admired, particularly that supreme novelist Wright Morris, and tried to draw me away from Henry James whose prose made him restless and frustrated. But more important than all of these acts of mentorship is the permanent seat he took in the audience I write for. It's a group of about ten or twelve, some imaginary, some long dead like Chekhov, Conrad, and Faulkner. Win sits in the front row, nodding thoughtfully over this phrase, looking doubtfully and sidewise at another, humming a little as he tamps down his pipe's ash, as he considers yet another. Even as I have worked on this essay, I have heard his gentle warning a couple of times, "Oh, come now."

We were to meet several times in New York City when he and El came east for short visits and rounds of theatre going. I stayed with them on two occasions after they moved to Santa Fe; the first time when I drove to Reno to acquire a divorce, and then in 1959 with my second wife and my oldest child. In the interim, in 1958, Win visited us in Hyde Park, where I had established a weekly newspaper and was living the kind of "bourgeois life" he was to describe of himself in a posthumously published memoir. He had come east at the invitation of New York University to conduct a summer poetry workshop, and he visited us for the July 4 weekend. He had just come from New Jersey. William Carlos Williams had invited him down to share the garrulous madness of Ezra Pound, just out of St. Elizabeth's and on his way back to Italy. Win bubbled over with anecdotes and the re-creation of that fellowship of two giants, and, implicitly, his acceptance within it. His attitude toward Pound was cool though amused.

Later, in 1964, after I had sold the newspaper and taken my family to Ireland to try to escape that bourgeois life, making my own form of exile, the Scott family met us in Dublin. They were on a cruise of Scandinavia and the British Isles, and their ship pulled in to Dublin for a day or two. We gave them a grand lunch at Jammet's Restaurant just across from Trinity College. Win was drinking more heavily, and he had gained an unhealthy weight. His roundish head seemed to have been stuck on a linebacker's neck, the shoulders had thickened, his whole stature rounded off. Ellie had chopped off her hair and looked flushed, angry. Her remarks had points in them that wounded in the guise of wit. Win appeared distant though he listened attentively as I compulsively talked about my writing. I was working on what was to become my "first" novel, typing every morning in the coal bin of the old row house we rented in Leeson Park. His thoughtful gaze above the napery and crystal soberly considered the summation I gave him of character and plot. But his look disheartened me, for he seemed disappointed; that my project fell short of his expectations—that he had come all this way, to this luncheon table in Dublin, Ireland, to hear such trivial stuff. That's what I thought then. Later I was to wonder if what I saw in his eyes was a toxic disappointment that ran in his veins.

Coinciding with the teaching appointment at New York University, was the appearance of his epic poem, *The Dark Sister,* published by NYU Press in 1958. The story was of Freydis, the half-sister of Leif Ericson who also had mounted an expedition to Vinland in search of timber. The poem had been on his desk for about ten years, had made the circuit of publishers for those ten years and had been the proposal for a couple of Guggenheims, both turned down. It was to be his major work, a summoning of his gifts for character and narrative, his canny feel for place, and all put together in the long-limbed cadence he had adapted from the old Icelandic sagas. *The*

Dark Sister seemed ready to become his so-called breakthrough. Malcolm Cowley, William Carlos Williams, Richard Eberhart wrote glowing reviews and responses. James Dickey in *The Sewanee Review* called it a masterpiece. William Jay Smith said it deserved a Pulitzer Prize.

But there was to be no Pulitzer, and the book disappeared without further notice. In 1959, Macmillan brought out *Scrimshaw* and again to excellent reviews by the likes of Gregory and Webster Schott. Even the usually cool *Kirkus* warmed up. Two years later, Doubleday published the essay collection *Exiles and Fabrications* and once more the work received high praise from the likes of Thornton Wilder and John Hutchens. Even the *New Yorker*. Then, Macmillan brought out *Collected Poems: 1937–1962* in 1962. On the short list for the National Book Award, the collection was barely reviewed— not even by the *New York Times*. What may have hurt Win even more was that, about then, some important alumnae of Brown had put his name up for an honorary degree, but the university establishment had vetoed the nomination—perhaps still smarting from those undergraduate attacks on compulsory chapel.

Thereafter, he was to publish two more volumes of poetry, *Change of Weather* in 1964 and *New and Selected Poems,* edited by George P. Elliot for Doubleday. Two posthumous works were to appear after his death from ethchlorvynol intoxication. Meanwhile, the novel I had tried to tell him about in Dublin was published by Macmillan in 1967 as *The Common Pasture.* Win called me from Santa Fe, bubbling with excitement and pleasure. I could visualize him standing in the living room, his eyes fixed on the Sangre de Christo mountains in the distance, pipe in one hand, as he congratulated me. A few days later, I received a letter that further refined his praise. He especially liked the old cowboy I had created, a broken-down rodeo rider hired for the opening celebration of a city mall. He praised the urban setting, its authentic reflection of the country's ills, he thought, and particularly the relationship I had pictured between the white and black communities. His forgiving eye singled out the good in that slim effort though he did quibble a little with the creaky melodrama of the novel's ending where the phony cowboy foils a bank robbery with only blanks in his six-gun. "Just a little bit too Hollywood, don't you think? But, maybe, that's all right."

Our letters and phone conversations in the last year of his life became more and more obsessed with the Vietnam War. The irreversible damage of that immoral enterprise made him distraught. His spirit and optimism had been permanently bruised by John Kennedy's assassination. How can we, as a people, he asked in a letter to me a couple of weeks after Dallas, "conclude in joy?" So, the Vietnam War only seemed to reinforce his darkest visions, and he publicly voiced his opposition in essays and letters to newspapers and journals. At times, he seemed to speak of the country's degeneration as if it were his own personal dysfunction—mind, body, and spirit.

One of the last conversations we had was early in 1968, just after Robert Kennedy announced his candidacy for the presidency. I had already promised to Kennedy what IOU's and influence I had acquired in New York State after a couple of campaigns for the New York Assembly. I chose to run, for a place in the convention delegation, against a very popular Democratic congressman who supported Johnson's policies and the war; but, mainly, the strategy was to keep Joe Resnick busy in the three or four mid-Hudson Valley counties we shared as a political base and therefore out of Kennedy's hair in the rest of the state. Popular history sometimes omits the fact that, before the California primary victory—and even after, it might be guessed— Robert Kennedy's candidacy was by no means a sure thing among New York Democrat politicos. He was, after all, an outsider in New York if not elsewhere!

Win was supporting Senator Gene McCarthy which did not surprise me. The image McCarthy projected as the intellectual-poet unwillingly dragged into the mire of politics, like Achilles from his tent, appealed to Win's model of the untarnished amateur in from the pond carrying some unique ideas. Of course, McCarthy was none of these. For me, Kennedy's power-wise and practical address of our urban and racial problems, his clear-eyed view of the Vietnam War, made him the only person who could restore us. And when he returned from the narrow victory in the Indiana primary, I thought I saw a greatness in him, tempered by that brutal and long-odds battle in which he experienced, probably for the first time, and certainly felt, for the first time, the common despair of the ordinary citizen.

In any event, Win and I good-naturedly argued our candidates' merits back and forth over the phone and by letter until Martin Luther King's assassination the first week of April. For Win, it was a gouging of that wound opened by John Kennedy's assassination; not just in his own psyche but in the body of the Republic. His equilibrium was put off-kilter. He began to drink more heavily and rage at wife and children. All the trust in the good lessons he had learned as a hardworking schoolboy in Newport and Haverhill, as a dutiful scholar at Brown, as a poet dedicated to his art— all that had come to dross. All the goals and all the rewards, bestowed or denied, must have been reduced to a joke.

When Ellie called me on the morning of April 28, my grief so shook me; I can remember shamelessly weeping into the phone, to such an extent that she ended up comforting me. (She would die herself only five years later in a tragic auto accident.)

My response had been, as much from anger as grief, a sense of betrayal by the gods who had denied me the joy of rewarding my mentor with a work I knew would please him. *An American Marriage* was an advance, I was sure, over *The Common Pasture;* moreover, it was a love story told in a voice that I had half borrowed from Win's. Compassionate, mildly self-deprecating but with a certain, ironic view of human aspiration and folly. Macmillan would publish the book in 1969, so Win would never see it, and this frustrating logistic had rushed into my mind as I talked with his widow. Suicide or accident, no one can be sure.

One more death was to come that spring of 1968—the one in Los Angeles on June 6—and all else would be a sorry anti-climax—the squandered soul of a nation, the sordid manipulation of a people.

In the final lines of the essay "Calendar for Santa Fe," from *Exiles and Fabrications,* Win wrote, "I shall go back (East) only after I have really settled." In the same essay, he questions the value of the high mesa desert outside the window. "Is this place too remote for human identification, too anti-human, too perfectly suited as the locale of the most anti-human weapon man has devised?" Did he mean to add, too distracting in its arid magnificence for a poet's work? A serious question for a poet whose life's work emphasized the human figure in place, the effect of one on the other. In any event, he never came back.

This question of place, this juggling of work and workplace, is the conundrum that challenges every young writer and one that will remain a puzzle on the last page of every unfinished manuscript. Fourteen books, years of commentary and opinion, scores of poems and essays and some of these among the treasures of American sensibility. Not such a bad record for one who sought liberation in exile. "Is exile the fabricator?" he asked in an essay, and as the best cicerones will not do, he gave no definitive answer. The question is more important than the answer. And so this morning, as with most mornings, I hear Win Scott's voice in my ear. "Leap."

1992

So Long, Natty Bumppo

Now that all the rivers have been named and the woods are dying, we look into the territory behind. Comfort is to be found in this old terrain, in the shadows that obscure the harsh reality of its crossing, and the hardships and the cruel events of our passage become separated in memory, romanticized. These woods are deep, and they have become a convenient dump for the embarrassments and wastes we don't wish to remember—it is a place for obscure burials.

In his presidential campaign of 1984, Walter Mondale reminded us of the hardships and sacrifices made in our past, suggesting that the same challenges should be confronted again, that the moral stamina within the national character was still sufficient to face up to a budget crisis and a suicidal arms race. It will be recalled that his review of these past sacrifices was found pretty uninteresting—even boring.

On the other hand, Ronald Reagan spoke only of the passage done. He suggested a journey through the woods and into a sunny savanna, and if there were shadows behind us, they assumed the mythic shapes of folk heroes who stood tall with clean hands and clear eyes, as all heroes must do. Instinctively, Reagan understood the American imagination needs these *recollections* of its history to be uncomplicated—no grime and no gore.

Our fortieth president's appeal was always attributed to his Hollywood image and to his actor's ability to communicate, but his canny insight into the American character, its unique attachment with the past—spurious or not—has always been underestimated. Not so much a creation of Hollywood, Ronald Reagan was more a persona sketched by Norman Rockwell—one of the more successful nostalgia-mongers in our cultural fabric. To review Rockwell's cast of characters as pictured on the covers of the *Saturday Evening Post* is to review some of the roles played by Reagan in the movies—the young baseball or football player doing his best, the kid getting his first physical examination, the draftee confronting the tough (but basically okay) top sergeant, the older, wiser and indulgent brother-uncle-sidekick-druggist-hometown pal—the sort of guy who listens to the problem and slips you the solution when no one is looking. Like Iran-Contra for example.

But whether Reagan thought being president was just another role to be played is unimportant; he wasn't the first nor will he be the last chief executive to think so and, besides, the majority of Americans think of the office as a place where the national character is supposed to be dramatized, acted out. In this respect, there may be subtleties to Bill Clinton's tenure that are yet to be appreciated. What made Reagan's performance so enjoyable, so applauded, were the allusions he made to a past that never existed—his projections of a metaphor for our history that omitted the incidents and personalities which would not fit on a Norman Rockwell cover.

It seems a majority of Americans saw through the role Reagan was playing but it didn't matter. They voted for him anyway. Polls following the first Mondale-Reagan debate gave Mondale the win by 56 percent, citing his superior knowledge of government, his ability to discuss and handle complicated issues, but the same percentile also said they would vote for Reagan. And they did.

He must be given credit for identifying and playing to the same kind of bifocal blindness that Lionel Trilling attributed to F. Scott Fitzgerald's characters—they fell for what they could see was false. "Possibly," Nick Carraway says of Gatsby, "it had occurred to him that the colossal significance of that light had now vanished forever." Yet, in the concluding lines of Fitzgerald's masterpiece, Carraway defines the fatal attraction of that light across the bay. "Gatsby believed in the green light, the orgiastic future that year by year recedes before us. So we beat on, boats against the current, borne back ceaselessly into the past."

Fitzgerald is not alone. Almost every important writer in the American anthology has explored this region we call our past. Hawthorne was sorry that it was not more complex—moonlight on the ruins and so forth—while James's people sifted through those ruins for something more acceptable to wear, something imported. Hemingway simplified the past, making it a virgin wilderness with clear waters to heal existential wounds while Faulkner put up No Trespassing signs, warning that the domain was dangerous and with treacherous light. It's a long list. But the first to post the boundaries was James Fenimore Cooper and his warden was Natty Bumppo.

It is a sorry example of Mark Twain's blind side—or maybe a sign of his envy—to see him poke fun at this tragic figure in his famous essay "Fenimore Cooper's Literary Offenses." We can't forget Twain's eager courtship of millionaires, the barons of American industry who bought up regions of our past to ravish their resources as they supported writers and presses that sentimentalized their histories. Yet, in that luminous moment on the raft when Huck Finn chooses not to return Jim to slavery, Twain was clear-eyed about the moral problem that goes with the territory, and if he mistakes the direction of that territory, as Wright Morris suggests others have, he must be revered for illuminating its major catastrophe.

We may still be going in the wrong direction, taking the most traveled and easiest path into a false wood, this pseudo yesteryear. Ronald Reagan was only one more actor putting on fringed leather to play Natty Bumppo to guide us around the ugly settlements, the rancid debris of the South Bronx. Chingachgook is no longer a wretched drunk nor even a savage whose name can be spoofed, but a harmless, tipsy Indian, posing for a Norman Rockwell or prancing in a Disney cartoon. Let us pause here to remember Sitting Bull, the great Sioux leader and foe of Custer, turned into a circus freak by William Cody's Wild West shows.

We Americans always seem ready to turn into the backlot of nostalgia—the territory behind. These stages of reconstructed memory offer a refuge from the awesome realities of this awful century's realties. As an audience we were well prepared to give Ronald Reagan standing ovations for his revision of the old days on the trail. We create fictions around the fears and frustrations we endure in our daily life—the pollutions of place, mind, and body that despoil us and the nuclear and biological pollutions that may ultimately exterminate us.

This withdrawal into "simpler times" has occurred across the cultural prairie. A diet of so-called *natural foods* assuredly has healthful values, as with most foods, but the mystique of eating nuts and berries carries a special persuasion. Similarly, the back-to-nature urgency of environmental campaigns may reflect a concern for our natural resources as it may also suggest a desire to turn away from the horrible environments we have made of our cities, and to leave them—sometimes in smoking ruins—for the suburbs and the unspoiled regions of our imagination where we can hike into a fantasy of roughing it like Natty Bumppo.

Small-town America has come back into fashion. This is not the small-town America that our poets and writers in the early part of the century rebuked for its hypocrisy, bigotry, and cruelty—places of spiritual death—but a cosmetized, sound-stage Hicksville complete with plastic pickle barrels. Sunbonnets made in Taiwan. The satisfaction of these constructions—in movies like *Pleasantville* and on TV and in popular novels—comes from the belief that these old regions have been cleared of their thorny problems, the moral and political issues that have lately choked our history.

Because, as an audience, *we've* come out all right. We've made it, so the sense is that if there were problems, they must have been solved. Beyond the wilderness, we can safely and enjoyably look back upon racism, political persecutions, and intolerance of every kind and consider them but shadowy fictions in a retrograde regionalism—like Reagan's television commercials.

After many years on the air, its popularity peaking during the Reagan era, the PBS radio program *A Prairie Home Companion* has installed the history of an imaginary village in northern Minnesota into our minds. Weekly, the genial host gives tours of Lake Wobegon, identifying its residents, dropping into the town café or the farm supply while recounting communal events. Folksy, humorous, and seemingly homespun, the narrative creates an image of a "little town that time forgot," as its creator and booster says, a place—if not a last resort—where a listener can escape the sophisticated banality and problems of contemporary life. *Our Town* has become our town.

A Prairie Home Companion is a good example of the new regionalism that embodies the same false nostalgia that appealed to Reagan voters and to all those angry, frustrated citizens who light up the control panels of call-in shows today. Keep it simple! There must be a simple solution to all the complexities we wake to in the morning or which have kept us awake all night. Somewhere in that papier-mâché wilderness the simple answer waits to be discovered. We can all remember the old days—in Lake Wobegon or elsewhere—when delinquency, misery, poverty—all human misery and chicanery had simple solutions. The woodshed and the washboard—anything that came between them would be straightened out, set right. And, as we have certainly learned in this awful century that is about to come to an end—one simple way to get rid of intolerance is to get rid of the objects of that intolerance. "For every problem, there is a simple solution," Mark Twain observed. "And it is usually wrong."

The great number of memoirs that have appeared lately might also be seen as a turn into the past, into memory, and it seems almost anyone's past, anyone's memory is worthy of review. To know the inside story of a personality has always been a curiosity to be scratched; it's one thing to read Plutarch, but Suetonius has the goods! However, currently our interests have been directed to the accounts of ordinary lives that often, in the convenience of their narrative circumstances, read like melodramatic novels. There is even some speculation that some of these books might have been novels in the first place but were converted by crafty agents and editors into "memoirs" in order to cash in on this current fad for plumbing the past—the so-called *real* past. Such expeditions, whether real or imagined, are merely treks into the sanitized woods already surveyed by *A Prairie Home Companion.*

American fiction has been unique in its emphasis on *place,* the dimensions, effect, and value of a place and how the neighborhood may reflect the spiritual or moral attitudes of its residents. "Do Nebraska," Henry James might well have said to a young Willa Cather as he had similarly advised Edith Wharton to look at her own territory of New York society. But today, too many contemporary American writers ride a smug fence line around a small plot that contains little more than their own staked-out self-pity. These dour caballeros are haunted by their own images caught in the surface of a backwater by Disney. It's not Natty Bumppo's fault! His signs were ignored and debased, but after so many false leads into the wrong territory we question the credentials of any guide.

Women, in one way or another—whether into convents or a room of their own—have often retreated from communities that kept them in menial positions or punished them for ambition, for endeavor—even for desire. For them, the good old days have been very few indeed, so their disengagement has been a method of survival while they regained their energies, found a new way through hostile territory. The view back from the Gender Gap may be a prospect from which we can find a better path for American politics and culture. Women poets and fiction writers seem to have no false nostalgia— save for a few memoirists here and there—and most of them confront the complacency of the settlement with a clear-eyed review of the real events of the passage. They report on the true nature of the outpost today. So perhaps a base camp has been established from which we may find our way out of this old-time melodrama and these old trails that go backward.

So long, Natty Bumppo—hello, Sacajawea!

1984–1998

Connections

It is "a fine feeling," M. F. K. Fisher notes, "to have a long-held belief confirmed. It adds a smug glow to life in general." But belief unconfirmed hardens into suspicions and becomes magnified in the cosmos of our misfortune, our bad luck. We make these sightings during solitary watches, connecting infinite fine lines like those drawn in astrological charts so they become the shapes of mythical beasts. Such cosmologies burn forever in the darkest outreach of our nightmares—surely, if not in the stars, our destinies lie in the faint connections we discover between them.

Even the dullest Rotarian perceives the importance of affiliations; understands how enlistment in one cause can advance one in another— the whole transaction having little to do with the merit of either party. These trade-offs are the stuff of minor memoirs, an archive of spurious fame, and my cold water flat on East 43rd Street was the site of such a revelation, though I do not remember if the bells of St. Agnes next door celebrated this nova. They seemed to ring pretty regularly and were, after all, dedicated to another cosmic event.

I do remember how it all began. Kraft dinner and five-cent avocados. In 1952, the packaged macaroni-and-cheese concoction cost fourteen cents a box. The overripe avocados were tricky to get back to the apartment all in one piece. I'd pick up these supper items on my way home from my job as a go-fer with a public relations firm whose clients were dance and concert artists: Martha Graham, Sylvia Marlowe, José Greco, William Warfield, and the pre-diva Leontyne Price among others. One of my jobs was to fill mail orders for a recording made by Lotte Lehman during one of her several farewell performances at Town Hall. My pay barely covered the eighteen-dollar monthly rent, food, and an occasional spree at some spa in Greenwich Village.

Others were doing better. One classmate was being paid twice what I was getting as a copyboy for the *New York Times,* but, in my opinion, the integrity of Corky's poetry was being suborned by the Ochs family, and— come to think of it—wasn't one of the Ochs daughters in our class? Hadn't she timidly toed around our off-campus Bohemian enclave in Providence, and—now, it all comes back—hadn't Corky walked her back to her dorm once or twice? Aha!

Meanwhile, I holed up in my cold and virtuous digs in the shadow of the Chrysler Building, turned on the electric heater and lit the oven, to write stories that I sent to the *New Yorker*. They always came back, but only recently someone had penned a personal note on the usual printed rejection form. Parts of the story had been "enjoyed" by some of the editors, it said, and I was encouraged to keep trying. But which parts had been enjoyed? Was it a matter of not enough parts or not enough editors enjoying the parts that there were? The ambiguity was stirred into many cups of instant Nescafe.

So when my mother blew into town from Philadelphia, where she taught at a small college, my own integrity, like Gogol's overcoat, was wearing thin and the winter was cold. My stomach was soured by near rotten fruit from a warmer clime. "Come to dinner with us," she said. "You'll enjoy meeting Rose."

"Who is Rose?" I ask.

"She was Gorki's last secretary. Or whatever." She rolls her eyes.

"You mean Gorki of *The Lower Depths?*" My question seems to challenge her, though not meaning to do so. She has looked away, around the Walgrens in Grand Central where we have met. It's near my apartment, and she's on her way downtown to stay with a friend in the Village.

"Well, maybe it was Trotsky," she says finally. "One of those people." Her hand waves at the entire Bolshevik pantheon.

How she met some of these people, I have never discovered. I suspect it was through the classified ads, advertising rooms for rent. Sometimes, in the 1930s, when I would join her in New York, I'd find her renting the back room of a railroad apartment that was jammed with Spanish-speaking refugees from Franco's fascist revolution. The manuscript of her dissertation at Columbia would be scattered over a narrow cot. I would sleep elsewhere, on a borrowed sofa or a friend's pullout. One time, her pinched alcove was reached through a kitchen where men and women plotted their return to Cuba, to join up with Sgt. Batista's revolution. What I'm saying is that the brand of the politics was of no importance to her; what was important was a place to sleep and a corner in which to write her thesis on Philip Freneau, the poet of the American Revolution.

The talk in all these places was as peppery as the aromas of the cooking; hectic, exotic accents that boiled up in language and stew pots and through which she would edge sidewise with the fixed graciousness of a tolerant tourist. So, I assume this mysterious Rose, last confidante or whatever to one of the Bolsheviks, was from the left wing of such a habitat, and the prospect of a meal in a restaurant, and a French restaurant at that, was too heavy a burden for my virtue to endure. I met them at Pierre au Tunnel that, in 1952, was located west of 8th Avenue in the 40s.

Recently, I have looked Rose up in reference books, her obituary appears in one of these, and I learn that she was the author of several children's books and had been a regular contributor to several magazines and newspapers, especially the *New York Herald Tribune Book Review*. She had been born in Rumania, but no reference is made to her political liaisons. Surprisingly, her birth date makes her four years my mother's senior, because the woman who looks up from the menu and takes my hand looks quite a bit younger. A soft cowl of coal-black hair encompasses a face whose dark, lustrous eyes look past my shoulder as my mother makes the introductions. These eyes review the plate rails of the dining room, then the candles on the tables, then the napkins and service china. It is a youthful, vagrant focus that takes in everything, everyone instantly, and wastes no time on irrelevant details.

Rose speaks with a schooled Oxonian accent that rests decently over a very foreign sound which sometimes rises to the surface of her speech and, when it does, she smiles engagingly as if to ask forbearance of this inadvertent reference to a different fluency, another life. She reminds me of those slightly untrustworthy and dangerous women I have come to appreciate in Hitchcock spy movies, so when I take the chair beside her, something happens to my breathing. I am sitting next to a woman who had typed manuscripts, or whatever, for men who had changed the history of the world.

"What wine will we have, Ellen?" she asks with an amused expression. She holds up the modest *carte du vin* but she handles it as though we might be dining at the Ritz. Her hands are small, the fingernails neatly manicured, clear polished.

"Oh, anything," my mother replies. Her lack of experience always made her an enthusiastic experimenter.

"I think this Beaujolais will do nicely," Rose says. The three syllables of the French unroll like a sunny hillside above the Rhone. "Let's have a whole bottle," she tells the waitress.

"Oh, my," my mother says.

Just as curious as to how these two women knew each other is the question of what the three of us are doing ordering *coc-au-vin* in this near empty, unpretentious bourgeois restaurant in mid-Manhattan.

"That sounds good," my mother has said. "I'll have that too."

What was the connection that brought us to this table? How did our stars come into this brief alignment, though by the time the salad was served—after the entrée in those days—it is clear that I have become the evening's focus? As usual, my mother has taken on the responsibility for the conversation, and the anecdotes of writers she had known, what this editor did to my father or that critic failed to say, have made Rose smile with a cool austerity. She has been directing more and more of her remarks toward me, a kind of casual test going on. Who have I been reading? What was I writing?

"Oh, just last month," my mother exclaims, "the *New Yorker* almost bought one of his stories."

"No, no," I quickly say. "Far from almost."

"Now, you know, Hilary, that's not true," she continues as if my modesty affronts her. "They wrote him a personal note and everything. Talked of how much they liked his work."

"That's wonderful," Rose says and leans toward me. Centuries of campfires glow in her gypsy eyes. I am sorry I have no secrets of any kind to pass on to her, no cause or government to betray. Yet, I am suffused with a well-being that goes from top to bottom as the rich meal settles in my belly. What an odd and wonderful life it is that seats a beautiful and probably dangerous woman at the same table with a young writer. Certainly this must be the sumptuous reward coming to me for those long, cold nights huddled beside the hum of the electric heater. The rejection slips collected in my desk drawer are being paid off, certificates of duty performed, compensation is being given for my solitary labor. And there's more to come.

One week later, a letter comes to me in the office mail. The return address is *The New York Herald Tribune Book Review*. A woman named Belle Rosenbaum inquires if I would be interested in reviewing books for them.

"Are you going to use your real name?" Corky asks me. I have just told him of my good luck as we have a beer at Minetta's Tavern in the Village. He has sighted the question with an eye lined up along his index finger. I'm the target.

"Why not?"

He laughs at something so very obvious that everyone in the bar except me must know, and in fact he looks around the place. No one seems to be listening. "Some people might make a connection. You know what I mean?" His speculation narrows his expression even more.

What my father did never made much difference to me until I moved east from Kansas City, until I determined that writing was to be my life's work. But since I had come to New York, I had—foolishly probably—stayed away from those places of employment, newspaper and magazine and book publishers—who might have given my application a special reading as the son of a famous poet. These days, it is all too common to see the son or daughter of a famous writer, using that connection to wedge a foot in a doorway while at the same time putting a knee into the parental groin—not such an impossible task as the rhetoric might suggest. And so what? What's the difference? Why not use the relationship if junior can write a line or two on his own?

But Corky's prosecutorial zeal has struck this vulnerable part in my integrity, or what I supposed was my integrity. Moreover, my confidence has been roughed up a bit by those *New Yorker* rejections that were become mice nests in my desk drawer. Further, Corky can remember, not so long ago, certain undergraduate beer sessions when I would reveal my ignorance about literature and this privileged information probably makes him laugh as we sit in Minetta's and I tell him that the *Herald Tribune* has asked me to review books. Surely, he is saying, it is not because of my command of literature. Clearly, we have come to a fork in our careers, low road and high, but, to be honest, I realize that I am not sorry either.

The review not only uses my real name in the by-line, but I have put in the middle initial as well. The article appears in the December 7, 1952, issue of the *Book Review,* and I am paid thirteen dollars and change. The only copy I have of this review is the one my mother framed and which she hung on the different walls of the different rooms she was to inhabit in the next forty years. The review reads not all that bad. That is, no cheesy odors of Kraft dinner, and the unsuspecting Sunday reader might think he was encountering the measured, judicious evaluation by a seasoned man of letters. The novel was found to be worthwhile though, regrettably, "a rather ordinary love-triangle" has been imposed on this view of small-town mid-America. "It seems unfortunate," the judgment rumbles, "that so much labor was devoted to the ordinary (that word again) drama of three worthless leading characters rather than to the rich potential of the supporting cast."

Did the night sky cleave open above East 43rd Street? I cannot remember. Phrases of such incandescence must surely burn away all ragged edges of the novitiate. I read the review over and over to the cockroaches. We found nothing to improve—not a word could be changed. No more dinners crafted from boxed, dry ingredients—I was about to join Edmund Wilson at the Century Club. In fact, I blow the whole check on fresh oranges, two steaks, and a bottle of Italian Swiss Colony red wine. Of course, the next time I see him, Corky never mentions my triumph. Minetta's is festooned with greasy Christmas decorations, a kind of celebration that seems appropriate, but I know he's seen the review—by-line, full name with initial.

When I think about it, I take his silence as a kind of warning to get my hubris under control; so, chastened I go back to macaroni and squishy avocados and to the typing of my own stories. I wear gloves, for January of 1953 is very cold in New York. Then, the season finally turns warm, and the bells of St. Agnes tune up for Easter, shaking the walls of my apartment with their tympani. Belle Rosenbaum asks me to do another book for them. It is a collection of stories called *The Enormous Radio and Other Stories.* The author is John Cheever.

If I could stop the narrative now to go back and make some revisions, do some tricky shifts of time and plot, would the narrative be different, the outcome of this muddle be changed? These long-held suspicions that harden into beliefs have a way of incorporating new evidence, even appropriating contrary theories into the ground of the original speculation. Indeed, speculation has always been more important than any proof—post-modern scientists are only discovering this for themselves. Speculation requires no proof and holy scriptures are successful in proportion to the number of ways they can be read. The true believer salvages whatever scraps he can find to build a shelter to keep his particular dogma dry.

"Let me tell you about Irita Van Doren," my mother tells me on the telephone. "She came from some dinky little school in the South to go to Columbia, and that was where she met Carl Van Doren. He was teaching composition or whatever in the graduate school. She was one of his students. When he left Columbia to go to the *Nation,* he took her with him. She sold advertising or something. Somewhere along the line, they got married. Then, when the opening on the *Herald Tribune* came about, he got her that job as editor of the *Book Review.* He was getting ready to dump her about then. Later on, she took up with Wendell Willkie. She wrote his speeches and so on. I hear she drinks."

"Oh yeah," I say. All this history has been prompted by the news of my second assignment. She has called me from Philadelphia to talk about a family matter, but her impulse for the anecdote has taken over.

"Oh, the Van Doren brothers made themselves very grand," she continues. "Every time your father and I would turn around, there would be Carl and Mark Van Doren. At Dreiser's parties, they'd show up. Hang around."

"Weren't they invited?"

"Of course, they were invited," she says after a moment, as if she might have gone over the guest list. "They were from Illinois, like your father, but you'd never know it."

This old history is of no interest to me. It is Belle Rosenbaum, Irita Van Doren's associate editor, who has asked me to review the Cheever collection. Yet, in an odd demonstration of how history may find its own goal, these worn and disparate skeins were woven into a design by a phone call one evening several years later. "What did I tell you?" my mother was to say.

Someone has called my wife and me to say that my brother was on television, had just been introduced on the program, *21* as the next challenger to the phenomenal Charles Van Doren, son of Mark Van Doren. Squeezed into his isolation booth like some gnomic oracle, young Charles had been accumulating piles of cash by answering questions on every subject to be found in an encyclopedia. But it is not my half-brother, but my cousin Dexter who materializes on our TV screen, and I wonder if the show's producers know the mistake or have purposely ignored the facts— stretched the relationship in order to announce this match as one poet's son going up against another. Or had Dexter misled the producers of *21*? My father sometimes complained that this nephew occasionally had identified himself as a son. Had there even been a casting call for poet's sons? And more important, *why* had Dexter stepped into the other isolation booth and slipped on headphones that guaranteed no improper coaching from the audience? As a founder of Consumers' Union, a pre-Nader advocate of honest advertising and fair product manufacture, what was he doing in this particular forum which, shortly thereafter, was to be exposed as a total fraud?

Because, when the scandal broke, it turned out that Charles Van Doren had known the answers all along; he had been schooled in his answers by the producers, as had some of his challengers, and, in fact, the quiz show and Charles Van Doren were brought down because one loser felt the payoff had not been sufficient, and he squealed. But what about cousin Dexter? He flunked the first round, misidentifying something by Brahms, as I remember. Did Dexter take a dive?

"There's something immoral about it," I am saying to my friend Nick Pileggi. His journalistic beat has uncovered the linkages between organized crime and so-called straight society, so he understands how pieces of string can sometimes tie up into interesting lengths.

It is now 1980 and we are eating big hamburgers in Costello's, a hangout in the east 40s for journalists from the *New York Daily News,* a few blocks over. Costello's used to be around the corner on Third Avenue, under the El, and a couple of blocks up from the cold-water flat where I typed up the stories I sent to the *New Yorker* and where I was reading John Cheever's collection sent to me by the *Herald Tribune* to review. In those days, I couldn't afford the menu, not even the hamburgers, but sometimes I'd drop in for a beer to appreciate the huge murals that James Thurber had drawn on the walls of the saloon; scenes of domestic anger and frustration, witnessed by quizzical animals. These same cartoons have been carefully transferred to the walls of the new location where Pileggi waits for me at a table. He is making notes on a folded sheaf of copy paper—he's always working.

When I lived on East 43rd Street, Nick was working as a copyboy for a wire service, later to become its New York correspondent and on his way to become the ultimate freelance journalist he is today. When I met him for lunch, he had helped found *New York Magazine* and is a regular contributor to its pages and other journals. As for me, when I join him at Costello's, I have published three novels and a handful of stories and I have started a weekly newspaper. I am working on a family memoir. So, the two of us haven't done so bad. "What's immoral?" he says, putting away his notes.

My morning mail has included a notice from the National Endowment for the Arts, telling me my application for a fellowship has been turned down once again. The NEA has also enclosed—perhaps a gesture meant to inspire collegiality—a list of those writers who were to receive $12,500 each—the prize then. The names of the judges are also given.

"Well, I note several poets connected with the St. Marks in the Bowery poetry project on the list, as well as some of the judges on the panel are also part of the St. Mark's business."

"What's wrong with that?" Nick asks. Pileggi has an indifferent way of asking such questions, as if he's not interested, which only provokes evidence and information to be volunteered.

"Because the work is supposed to be judged anonymously, on its merits alone. What if a group of editors and writers take turns as judges, awarding each other grants?"

"Does that happen?"

To apply for a grant is humiliating enough—it picks at the onus almost every artist carries around—not to be an entirely self-supporting, first-class citizen and taxpayer. But to suspect the procedure has been rigged, by fellow artists, so that certain people already know the answers, like Charlie Van Doren, riles a bitterness that I'm trying to wash down with a swallow of Guiness.

Nick is carefully cutting his hamburger into manageable sections. His expression is fixed as he works the knife and fork, a kind of *commedia dell'arte* smile on him that indicates he is listening but also turning over the different possibilities of my complaint. Years later, after the NEA rules were changed to make the procedure fairer, largely due to this lunch with Pileggi, a poet boasted to me that the Fellowship was a "crap shoot," though his own roll of the dice had just turned up lucky for a second time.

As long as writers, editors, and publishers make up a panel that will hand out large chunks of money—the current prize is up to twenty thousand dollars—the possibility of logrolling cannot be discounted. A true lottery would give every writer an equal chance. A true lottery would eliminate juries entirely. Why not use social security numbers, anonymously on file with the IRS, and each year a computer would make a random selection from this pool? True, the work's merit would be ignored, but this is a subjective evaluation in question from the beginning when the program began in 1964. My own outrage is picking up heat in the smoky, noisy ambiance of Costello's.

"Well, so what?" Nick says and uses his napkin.

"What do you mean?"

"What's so new about these deals? The Guggenheim does it. The Pulitzer and the National Book Award have been known to be swapped around. Everyone knows about that. How is this any different?"

It is different, I want to say, because it has just happened to me. My name has not been swapped around and does not appear on this list I got in the mail this morning. That's the difference. I had hoped for a grant to finish the memoir I was working on, a sample of which had accompanied my application. Pileggi's eyes have a humorous glow in them which suggests he's come up with the same answer, the same sorry fact. Then, I hear myself say, "We're talking about taxpayers' money with this one; not the interest on the estate of some guy who went down on the *Titanic*. These are monies raised by Congress and supposedly awarded on the basis of merit and not because of somebody's connections." Do I sound like Jesse Helms?

Nick sits back in his chair, suddenly serious. "Why don't you do a piece on it," he says.

"Do a piece?"

"Sure, make some calls, do the research, see if your suspicions have any facts out there. Do a piece. For the magazine. For *New York*."

The Enormous Radio and Other Stories by John Cheever (235 pages, Funk and Wagnalls, $3.50) is a collection of fourteen stories, many of them first published in the *New Yorker*. I have already read some of them in those pages. Together with John O'Hara's, Cheever's work epitomized the *New Yorker* story for me—both writers clearly outsiders, an identity I put up and preserved in the cool rooms next to St. Agnes. Cheever's wry dissection of the weary inhabitants of the Upper East Side has especially enforced my own view of this class from my vantage point on East 43rd Street. How his cold scalpel laid open these empty lives sometimes warmed me as I waited for the macaroni water to boil. His eye for detail, his ear for the nuance in a dialogue and that special use of the fantastic in the midst of Chekhovian realism, as in the title story, were gifts I tried to pass on unsuccessfully as my own to the editors of the *New Yorker*. So now, Belle Rosenbaum has given me an opportunity every apprentice dreams of—to offer public praise of one's master. A glorious transcendence has settled upon me.

After a leisurely lunch at the Century, Bunny Wilson and I would go our separate ways. I would look up Cheever, perhaps at McSorleys way downtown, a place with just a gloss of elitism wiped across its working-class history, as the sawdust on the floor dusted the gleam of polished loafers. Cheever would be sitting at a corner table, surrounded by friends—a few younger fellows like myself sitting on the fringe. When I sit down, a flicker in the hooded eyes, or so they appear in the bookflap photo, will signal his recognition. The others have not noticed. Later, I find myself standing next to him at the bar.

—Whom have you been reading? he'll ask. A companionable, professional question. An exchange among near equals. While I'm thinking up an answer, Cheever has turned to a man standing next to him.—Oh, Bill, I want you to meet young Masters, who wrote that extraordinarily perceptive review in the *New York Herald Tribune*.

—Hello, Mr. Styron, I'll say. I certainly enjoyed *Lie Down In Darkness*.

—What are you writing these days? Styron will ask and both authors lean forward, intent on my answer.

"I'd like you to read the collection over again," Belle Rosenbaum is saying. She has called me at my job—Lotte Lehman's penultimate farewell is still doing okay—to say the review she received from me wasn't exactly what she wanted. "John Cheever is one of my favorite writers," she says. "I like him very much."

"He's one of mine too," I protest. "I like his work very much, but this collection all together—well."

"Try reading the stories again," she says, "and see if you may have a different opinion." Her voice is patient, the tone of a kindergarten teacher helping a charge through some basic endeavor.

"Actually, I read the whole collection a couple of times," I say and this was true. My review had surprised me as apparently it has disappointed the book review editor. Maybe something in the air the night I wrote it out; perhaps, something sour in my stomach might have tainted my appreciation.

Rosenbaum's voice implies she may have made a mistake entrusting John Cheever to such an unknowing lout; obviously, a mistake she would not make again. I could hear the heavy doors of the Century Club closing on the golden associations within. So, I went home that night and reread the whole collection.

So much, for now, of 1953. What about 1980? Certainly, my questioning of the NEA Fellowships was prompted by my own sense of slight—a point that some, including a meanly edited interview on *All Things Considered,* made without really addressing the substance of the article or the questions it raised when it finally did appear. For when has reform or, even, revolution ever been born of the satisfied or inspired by those on the approved list? The question of motivation is pointless. My research seemed to confirm my suspicions, and every phone call enlarged the scope of the inquiry. One contact led to another from New York to California to Minnesota to Rhode Island to Massachusetts to Louisiana—a network of phone interviews that supported my suspicion that many of the awards had been rigged. If it was a conspiracy, it was nationwide, not just a few trade-offs by the bunch down at St. Marks in the Bowery. "Go Down Dignified" is on the record, and its findings are too extensive to include here. But one finding might be looked at as synecdochial.

In addition to many instances of grants given to authors by their own editors or publishers acting as panel judges, and in addition to several so-called household awards where couples doubled their take—a probability hard to reproduce in any crap game—one very startling pattern emerged. Ten percent of the 1979 Fellowships were given to authors published by five or six small presses, most of which did not accept unsolicited manuscripts—and these same presses were represented on the panel of judges by editors, publishers, and in-house authors of these same presses. In effect, by subsidizing these particular authors, the government was also subsidizing the presses that published this solicited work, making up a tidy little circle of what some might call a "vanity" publishing network. And all paid for with public monies. So, where was the choice by merit?

However, the scope of the article had gone beyond the city limits of *New York Magazine.* The young editor who had been overseeing the article became perplexed, for the pieces of string had tied together into a ball larger than I had anticipated, so the magazine paid my four-hundred-dollar phone bill and gave me a generous kill fee. Nick Pileggi called Lewis Latham at *Harper's* about the piece and he read it, expressed sympathy for some of the findings but eventually backed off. Victor Navasky of the *Nation* didn't think there was anything wrong with editors helping out their authors, and the article was too long for them anyway. Meanwhile, someone had xeroxed the piece and copies began to circulate among the literati. Sections of it were quoted at summer writing colonies. Eventually, the editor of the *Georgia Review* asked to read it, and "Go Down Dignified" (from the Robert Frost poem) was published in the summer issue of 1981.

Well, what went wrong? Belle Rosenbaum says, "Try it again."

"I've read the stories a couple of times," I tell her. "Some I had read already in the magazine."

"Try them again," she says.

My mother never gets to frame this review, for it was never to be published. So, I cannot call up exactly what I said, or even what I was supposed to say. Dutifully, I returned to my apartment that evening and reread *The Enormous Radio,* painfully aware of the connection between my future with the *Book Review* and my opinion of the stories. If I cannot recall the exact wording of that opinion, I can easily summon up the mood that overcame me as I reviewed that opinion, for I would have the same response today. How few of us can alter the vision we have of ourselves, of our place in the Hall of Virtue? If anything, we merely change lenses for a more acute definition of the same perspective. I can imagine the self-righteousness that overwhelmed my good sense.

More than my career with the *Herald Tribune* was on the line, I told myself. Free speech—*my* free speech was being threatened. Belle Rosenbaum had decided I was adequate to judge the work of an unranked Midwestern novelist, but obviously I was not up to the demands of a writer who appeared regularly in the handbook of the Eastern Establishment! Where, in fact, my own work had almost been accepted, let it be remembered!

And what had I said in this review of Cheever's stories? I would be cruelly reminded of my own opinion as other reviews appeared in different journals and book pages. Most of us said the same thing—that the stories were sharp insights into these particular urban strata, but read as a collection, their view became narrow, the characters more obvious and the technique less surprising. Whit Burnett in *Story No 3* put it most diplomatically. " . . . In the aggregate they present a rather overwhelming picture not for sustained reading from cover to cover." Arthur Mizener went to the other extreme of the same opinion in the *New Republic.* "Taken at one sitting, the fiction machine is more in evidence. (Cheever) is not a writer of great talent."

That is pretty stiff. I cannot agree with Mizener. My response was more along the lines of William Du Bois in the Books of the Times of May 1, 1953. "The melancholy fact remains that a little of Cheever can go a long way. Like all special formulas, his is most effective when taken in small doses—preferably in single installments, with plenty of Addams and Arno in between. Fourteen Cheevers taken in sequence could conceivably be a lethal dose for the too-sensitive reader."

DuBois's sentiments were so similar to mine that I clipped out his review and sent it to Belle Rosenbaum. The orange highlighting of my grease pencil has become even more garish as the old newsprint has yellowed, for Rosenbaum returned it to me. See? I must have said in some fashion or other—look at what the *New York Times* said. "I had thought of sending *you* this clipping," she wrote back. "He doesn't like the book either but it is the manner and method of saying that counts."

The manner and method of saying it. I study Talliferro Boatright's review in the *Herald Tribune Book Review* of May 24 to see his manner and method. His opinion was the same as mine but he does show good manners in his method. His respect for Cheever's picture of "lives in the 50's or higher on the East Side" (where he announces his own citizenry) is clearly evidenced. Perhaps, I did not show enough respect.

Now what is this entire muddle about? Not only have I digressed, as Montaigne would have said several times over by now, but this wrangle of soiled linen, this press of sour grapes has become a potage of old histories and sullen narratives. *Que sais-je,* the spirit of the master nudges me to ask, and what do I know indeed? What have I found out about myself? Surely the reader is entitled to more than this posturing vanity, this indecent exposure, indecently exposed? What's the connection, Pileggi would ask, a merry flash in his Calabrian eyes.

"What passes for morality these days," George Garrett wrote a while back, "is often more a matter of fear (in disguise) than virtue." Plato warned us of poets, but he forgot to tell us about the sons of poets—or even the nephews of poets—who appear before millions as the petitioners of truth and knowledge, keepers of honest flames. Did the revelation of Van Doren's televised fraud, and the moral discouragement it produced, prepare us for others—say, the spiritual bankruptcy of Vietnam? Our American dishonesty—the complimentary picture we have of ourselves—has been so attractively packaged and illustrated from the covers of the *Saturday Evening Post* to the booths of TV quiz shows to the shores of Lake Wobegon that we may have been conditioned to even greater falsehoods. Watergate. The Iran-Contra conspiracy. Most of what has passed for political leadership in the last several decades. Why, then should we ask higher standards of our poets and writers—eager as they are to join the Rotarian fellowship of the American Academy or the rotating academies of the different fellowships—they are only human and Americans as well?

To be useful, let me take down the plastic sheeting on these windows that overlook East 43rd Street. The warmth of June rises from the pavements and bounces off the facade of the Chrysler Building. It is a new season, warm and full of hope. One afternoon, on my way home from work, I deliver some photographs to the *New York Times* of the harpsichordist Sylvia Marlowe. I think she may have been doing a concert of Stravinsky with her quartet at the Little Carnegie Hall about then. I run into Corky. He's through work also and we decide to go around to the China Bowl off of Times Square for some chop suey and a beer.

The last time we met at Minetta's, he never said anything about the Cheever review—that it had not appeared—nor about the one by Boatright that had. I appreciate his discretion. In fact, his silence has surprised me. But then, he looks up from his noodles and says, "That was a nice ad in the *Herald Tribune Book Review.*"

"What ad was that?" I pictured an ad for *The Enormous Radio* with quotes from some of its reviews.

"That ad for the dictionary," Corky says. "You know." He winks and laughs a little, very pleased by something. "A full-page ad for *Webster's Collegiate.*"

"So what?"

"Well, Funk and Wagnalls publishes the *Webster's Collegiate,* right?" I stare across the red Formica tabletop as Corky aims a finger at me, sights down its length. "And who put out your man's book? Funk and Wagnalls, wasn't it?"

That all-knowing, IRA aim of his look pierces me to this day. I can still see him, laughing at the exposure of my naïveté—once more, my ignorance shown off in all its dumbness. I admit to looking for that ad for *Webster's Collegiate Dictionary.* Once or twice I have spun through the microfiche files of a library, reeling through weeks and months of the *Herald Tribune Book Review,* but I have not yet found it. Which doesn't mean it is not there. Somewhere. Somewhere, in the stars, there's a connection.

1993

A Day in Burgundy

This morning I left St. Symphorien-de-Lay to meet the Loire just south of Roanne, and I will follow this beautiful river up to Digoin, a distance of about sixty kilometers on Route D982. It has been a lovely day in Burgundy. June weather in France. The dense aroma of ripening fields as their green and yellow carpets of trefoil and wheat unfold in the sunlight to be caressed by the shadows of close-flying cumulus clouds.

In the distance, low-slung farmhouses in the manner of old Roman villas, some with red-tiled roofs—some might very well be old Roman villas. Then, my little Ford is abruptly enclosed by a village. Buildings and high walls make a narrow corridor of the route, their clay surfaces reinforced by pebbles, called "pierres dorees" because of their yellowish luster. At one corner, the knife-sharp edge of a townhouse projects like the prow of a stone ship, as if becalmed centuries back. It could cut me in two if a strong enough wind came up, so I carefully steer around it and come into the neat, open space of the village's square with its ubiquitous tablet dedicated to "les enfants de la patrie." A farmer in a blue jacket and cap, and wearing high, black work boots, marches resolutely across the space toward the village's three or four stores, a *poste* and a *tabac,* lined up on the far side of the square. He is a countryman, French and therefore a realist so does not recognize the catastrophe that might have happened to me at the corner behind him. Then, just as suddenly, I am back in the open countryside.

Since leaving Italy, many of these small French towns have tempted me to linger in them and snoop about their byways. Each one, according to my guidebook, offers an item for the serious tourist; a church with an interesting Ascension on its tympannium, something remarkable on another's lintel or a pleasing view of a chateau (not open to the public) where a twelfth-century abbot of Cluny was born. But I am traveling not sightseeing; I stop only for meals and sleep. Yet, I am in no hurry. The wand of the speedometer rarely rises to the red line, and I have no particular schedule, but loaf a little closer each day toward Luxembourg from where my return flight to America departs. The curiosities, the historic sites en route cannot tempt me—I am my own tourist.

Strange to go for days without conversation. Can one get out of practice talking; forget how to shape the sounds and assemble them into meaningful sentences? Something more than mere communication. Of course, I have ordered meals and asked for a room at night, but these exchanges exercised only a utilitarian grammar, a Berlitz fluency that evaporated like the morning dew on the hood of my car. With little ceremony, a concierge or a waiter tactfully restored my isolation to me, and though a storekeeper's eyes might suddenly glisten with interest, it is also clear to her that I am a traveler off the track and nearly out of season. She holds back her curiosity.

So, I make this journey within the three containers of my small car, my lack of language, and my mind. But, these restrictions also grant me a curious freedom of speculation and an open range of thought; a liberty of movement within memory and imagination that has no limits though I may never get anywhere. This habit of mine to seek solitude within a community has left many behind; lovers and children, all paradoxically exiled on their own home turf. I have viewed them from afar, from the road that turns within me, and though some are very attractive, I do not often tarry.

My time in Italy might have caused the curious pilgrimage I am now making in France. From my base camp in Radda in Chianti, I made forays into Volterra, Sienna, Florence, and places in between. Images were collected; my journal grew fat with observations. Some of its pages even press wildflowers picked in the fields. I worked hard to speak the language within the high walls of medieval hill towns. I became clotted with pasta and Michelangelo. I gorged on the postures of chic *florentina* who, in the burst of a Vespa, become deliciously practical as they hopped on the seats behind their boyfriends. The ceramic miens of Etruscan couples soothed me as they lounged on their tomb lids, waiting for passage to that All-Night Banquet. So, I have a satchel full of menus, and I have made the rounds. I have explored the vestibules and wings of the museum that is Tuscany.

The evening before I leave Italy, I open this letter in the garden of the fattoria where I stay and read my daughter's angry words in the amber light of twilight. The dramatic light on the hills beyond and around this vineyard limns the same flatness of background that Martini and Giovanni di Paolo painted with such exquisite exactness in the fourteenth century. Their ignorance or even contempt for perspective made them realists—this is the way the landscape looks! My daughter's words tear at my heart, and, so for relief, I have looked away to locate myself in this landscape, for its appearance has never changed. Her attack questions our whole history and my affection for her. I am mystified and hurt, especially because, lately, I have been her only advocate within the family. Something I have written her has caused this outburst—my words, in the arc of their posting, have fallen short of their meaning, my intention. A misconstruction has occurred; yet, her unstoppered fury is so intense as to suggest a long-endured ferment, a wounding that has never healed. Our relationship has not been what it has seemed.

My last evening in Radda, in Italy, I dine at a local tratorria called Miranda's. It is a picturesque place and has become a regular stopover for package tours. When I arrive several huge buses are already parked before the restaurant, their engines patiently digesting their essence, as their passengers dig into the *tipico cucina* inside. English and German diners or so the origin tags on the rear end of the buses indicate.

The place is entered through the kitchen where women of several generations prepare vegetables, wash dishes, attend pots on the large black stove. Miranda, an overblown version of the actress Colleen Dewhurst, conducts me to a small corner table and takes my order. Carefully, I recite my rehearsed Italian, for I wish to set myself apart from the other patrons who stick to their own languages. They ask for "green salad" or "kase"— some merely point at the menu items. The English seem amused by their own arrogance, but I think I detect a kind of surliness in the Germans' tone. You Italians, they seem to imply, must remember a little German from the last time we were through here in 1944. But the language we speak doesn't seem to matter to the help.

From my table, I can look directly into one corner of the kitchen where two women wash dishes at a large slate sink. A third woman fills plastic bottles with water from the tap. These bottles all bear the labels of popular mineral waters; Fuggi, Panna—and for those diners who prefer the sparkling spring water of the French Alps—Evian. Similarly, a fourth woman decants wine from a raffia-wrapped jug into funnels inserted into bottles with labels that correspond to the *listi dei vini*. Whether Barolo Mascarello or Chianti Ruffino, it's all the same wine but priced appropriately to each bottle's label.

An English couple circumspectly objects to their Barbaresco San Lorenzo arriving at table already uncorked. But the waitress, a demure child whose features might have been sketched in by Donatello, pours the stuff and waits patiently for them to order their meal. It is a lesson that Italy teaches the naive and unwary; we all get the same fare, no matter how fluently we might order something else.

But it is an old lesson, and I am weary of its teaching. By *dolchi*, I am more than ready to leave Italy and this table. The rigid routine of *antipasto, primo,* and *secondo* has become oppressive. Standardized. The historic guile has made me impatient and the uniformity of facades has blanked out my interest. The square, marble fronts slapped onto rude brick churches are like the ornate faces of old western emporiums nailed together to promote the hardware or the ecstasy to be found inside.

So, for several days I have been drifting through France, aimlessly choosing each fork in the road, making random selections from menus; once, sharing the *plat du jour* at a truck drivers' *relais.* I don't have to work hard at the language here in France; on the contrary, I seem to have become speechless, embrace a self-perpetuating silence as I noodle along toward Digoin. My child's letter lies in my pocket, and I am trying to sort out the circumstances of this painful rupture, this misunderstanding. To order ideas and then to express them requires a mind disciplined to discern differences. No labels are needed. Human thought implicates a self, but this self often becomes self-important and gets in the way of clear thinking, genuine feeling. It wants to be noticed. Perhaps, I have committed this folly? My sense of my self as "the father" may have only addressed her, put the imprint of this persona on the exchange rather than speaking directly to her in a simple fluency learned by the heart. I may have made myself extrinsic to her concerns.

Lately, I have been thinking of the computer as an extrapolation of this self, or as close as mathematics can get to it—this externalization of the human mind. On the road to Digoin, I have opened this file, if you will, in order to avoid my daughter's letter, in the same way I had looked away toward the Tuscan hillsides. Shouldn't we be a little wary of this linguistic instrument taking over the mind's meanderings, the self's playful associations of ideas and impressions? Soul's work. This electronic, booted-up tool of materialism would much impress Locke and his gang, but isn't it one more device to separate mind from self, from soul? And what a beguiling trick we may have played upon ourselves, for, with the flick of a switch, we have become the passive audience of our own conceits, as we install a governor on the half-wake, half-dream mind that has been free-wheeling, if not free-willing me down Route D982.

The Loire joins the Arroux at Digoin, and I am offered a choice of four roads to take; one due east to Macon, two to the left that accompany the Loire's westerly bend, and a northern route that strikes out along the banks of the Arroux. My Ford homes in on this one, Route D994, with Autun about seventy kilometers ahead. A likely spot for a picnic lunch. Fields of grain still play out on either side of the road but, here and there, the staves of vineyards begin to offer more static chords. A purplish blur has appeared in the left corner of my windshield. Le Morvan, my map indicates.

This geological wonder rises nearly three thousand feet and covers thirteen hundred square miles of forests, rocky gorges, and fast-running streams. The road, like all French roads, is clearly marked and well maintained. The air is fresh. The Ford hums. My destination is plainly before me.

Not all my excursions in Italy were made to the usual tourist sites. I also poked into the dusty corners inside my head, a storehouse of useless artifacts and unverified illusions, and these tours were often guided by William Barrett's *Death of the Soul,* a book I had packed in my duffel. His witty discourse with Kant, and particularly his references to the computer, has encouraged my own awkward grabs at the ultimate question. The final disgrace. How can the infinite mind transcend, go beyond what might be called its finite predicament? The original how-come question. The cruel paradox given us by the same Folks who brought us the Big Bang and to which the ingenious orthodoxy of the computer seems to offer a solution. To keep memory accessible forever might be the long-sought answer.

Barrett describes a spider spinning its web outside a window of his study. He wonders what kind of mind the spider has, the nature of its consciousness. "We humans are farther along the scale of evolution, perhaps, but in our own way we are as finite and our mind as attached to its own conditions as the spider's to its own. We spin the brilliant web of our scientific concepts, but we cannot step beyond it." We *impose* (a favorite Kantian usage) our imaginations, our soul's yearnings upon the material, finite world to create models of paradise such as St Mark's, or to construct the imperishable luminosity of poetry, or to seek the split-second salvation of orgasm. But now, with the computer, we can put up the reflection of our genius on screens, store them in eternal memory banks to achieve a kind of secular deliverance and resurrection of that genius. That's the idea.

The direction taken by the soul's eternal life is all-important. The Greeks and Romans and others seem to go underground but Christianity has always gone up, true believers winging after Jesus—the first Big Bird—on His flight heavenward. And, so on. Some of this metaphor's success must be due to the envy all earthbound creatures have of birds' flight, but only humans were given the understanding, with its concomitant pathos, as to why we cannot get off the ground. We are heavier than our imaginations, and the revolutions of the globe keep us pinned within the smothering embrace of mother earth. Without this reasoning of the problem, Icarus would have remained an unknown malcontent and the Wright Brothers would have stuck to bicycles. There'd be no interesting Ascensions to check out over tympanniums.

But now we are going in a different direction—out. Outside and into the ethos. The mind radiates into a kind of all-embracing mimesis that, if it does not offer salvation, seems to guarantee a place of eternal salvage. Computer networks are becoming celestial dumps where the faithful can be uploaded forever and ever. Amen, if not hallelujah. But, like Barrett's spider, have we only just spun another fine web which, with all its fabulous constructions and glowing synapses, still limits us, keeps us earthbound, passive worshipers as we hack away at our own reflections? The mind may be put on file forever on the Internet, but the soul is left behind because it cannot be described—not even Plato, nor anyone since, could program it—so this inner self, with all its pitiful awareness of its container's vulnerability, is left behind. All the old-time religions, at the very least, promised we could take the soul along—no matter in what direction we were destined to go—but there's no room for it on the hard drive.

As I near Autun, the shadow on my windshield has enlarged, the blues have deeply purpled with patches of bright greens and granite gray, and the scale of the Morvan Massif becomes even more dramatic as the flat terrain of the Arroux basin runs ahead to abruptly meet its wall. The three-thousand-foot Haut-Folin rises like a huge dam on my left, and for the second time this morning, I feel a little threatened, but the great sea that lay behind this huge extrusion has drained into the Seine basin long ago, and I safely enter Autun. If I had looked away and had not seen it, would this enormous upheaval of granite really exist? Or say, once observed, did my eyes give the topography its marvelous colors? Is this mass only an arrangement of grays? No such philosophical whimsies can qualify the existence of my daughter's letter. It lies in my jacket's pocket to be read again and again, to replicate its anguish and anger.

Autun is noted for its Romanesque treasures, but I ignore them, according to my new habit, and set up my picnic in the Roman theatre near the old town walls. I put down the items of my lunch on the worn stone seats of what might have been the "family circle," if the Romans had such a ticket. The roasted half-chicken I picked up in Digoin is still warm and fragrant with tarragon and lemon. The small round of chèvre and the pear take up a pleasing sonata of forms in the open air. When I break into the crusty demi-baguette, I hear the cheerful greeting of the proprietor in Gueugnon, a half-hour ago, when I opened the door of her *boulangerie*. "Bon Jour, m'sieur!" The half-drunk Rhone, left over and corked from yesterday's picnic near Valence, has come into its own while rolling about the backseat of the car.

I imagine the Romans, fifteen thousand of them according to the Michelin Guide, leaning forward in these seats to catch the bawdy fun of a road company doing Plautus. But then at play's end they would emerge from this theatre into Gaul—not Rome. For a couple of hours, they could believe they were in the center of the Empire, of their universe; yet, how sad they must have become, how keen their feeling of exile, as they came to their senses on the walk home. To refer to W. C. Fields—an authority that Plautus would certainly have respected—it would have been similar to coming out of Olivier's "Hamlet" to find you were still in Philadelphia. Augustus founded this city (he gave it his name, *Augustodunum*) and his intent was to build a sister city to Rome, a reproduction of his Imperial Capital. This theatre, for example, was the largest one in all of Gaul.

So no matter its grandeur, this colonial outpost was still only a copy, an imitation of the original and, in fact, one put down in hostile territory. The Roman impulse to press its own image on a conquered land is not all that different from the self imposing its character on a child's mind or the mind booting up its self-definition on an electronic tabula rasa which, if it is the ultimate tool of materialism, surely must be the ultimate vanity mirror. The motivation of all colonialism is to duplicate and therefore perpetuate the parent consciousness, filtered through the ego. Plautus wrote of this obsession—so did Milton and Dickens. O'Neill. It's a long list.

Some years ago, my wife, another child, and I drove from New York to Santa Fe, New Mexico. Several days out we stopped off to visit friends who had moved to a small town in southern Illinois. All day we had driven through fields of soybean and corn, punctuated by the bobbing heads of oil rigs, bringing up the residue of other, ancient vegetation. Near evening, we pulled into this dilapidated village by the tracks of the Wabash Railroad. The hamlet's several stores leaned into each other and a two-pump gas station starkly glared out from beneath a bay illuminated by bare bulbs. Across the street, an empty bank dared the ghosts of the Barrow Gang. A battlement of enormous grain silos rose from across the railroad tracks. From miles away, these gigantic constructions give the unknowing traveler the impression that a prairie metropolis lies just ahead, a place with all the amenities of civilization, but close up, these concrete, eyeless volumes usually reign over near deserted junctions of road and rail like the temples of a vanished race—of a people that had outgrown their ability to feed themselves.

Our friends live in a large, rambling house built across the tracks from these silos by the man who had owned the local lumber mill—neither now in business. They keep a peculiar squalor, a kind of disinterested dishevelment that indicates an indifference to the usual routines of daily life and housekeeping. He is a sculptor but works as a draftsman in a nearby plant that designs and manufactures electronic devices for missiles. But this is only a job, for, it is clear his real work takes place in a second-floor bedroom, overlooking their backyard, the railroad tracks, and the silos.

He is a mathematician-sculptor, and in this back room he is piecing together the model of a conception that is to rise from these plains and equal—no, exceed the size of the silos outside the window. "It is to be an art form that is not to be viewed objectively," he tells us. "Nor from without time, but which the viewer steps into and views from within. Consequently, the art changes with the viewer and time of its perception." He wants to enclose the whole town. Maybe more, his eyes suggest.

This construction takes up the entire room, the whole cubic volume of its space, and to view it "properly," we must fit ourselves within it. The sculpture is made of metal pipe, plastic sheets, pieces of mirror and colored vinyl scraps and patches; like a playground's maze and our daughter responds appropriately, her spirits rise. It has been a long day for her in the cramped seat of the car. But no artistic whimsy has produced this work. Every fuse of plastic to metal, every joint of aluminum tubing, each placement of clear and colored segments, every positioning of mirror has been posited and proved by a mathematical formula. Pages of algebraic computations lie scattered about the floor like the wrappings of an enormous gift.

When built, the actual prototype will rise above the silos; whole communities are supposed live within it, and every citizen can view the relationships of planes and angles and surfaces from inside. In effect, they will be living within its creator's mind, observing, perhaps subjectively evaluating how his intellect worked out the different problems presented by his imagination, his speculation. They would be impressed and enclosed by his concept, his premise, in the same way these playgoers, two thousand years ago, were held within the imperial vision of Rome, no matter how they responded to the comedy before them. Our friend hoped to extrude himself by this jackstraw assembly that would impose a model of his soul, mathematically proved, upon this Illinois plain. It would be a sort of Hegelian proof of himself and much better than one formulated in concrete or stone because it would be continuously renewed, reborn and worked out, by the generations living within it.

Outside the window, the conical roofs of the grain silos had turned orange with the light fleeing west across the prairie and toward a horizon that pulled the rail lines together into a single thread. Farm boys clustered outside the lighted window of a barbecue café. It was a scene out of Wright Morris, and we could have been in the presence of genius here in this room also. Our daughter had become attentive, quiet. Here in Autun, only this theatre, a couple of gates, and some rubble of the old wall remain of that Roman city. The grand vision has been pillaged and appropriated into later models of human ambition.

So, I clean up my area of the old theatre, get into the Ford, and continue my journey through one of these two last gates, now called Port d'Arroux. Two handsome arches for vehicles flanked by two smaller ones for pedestrians—those Romans thought of almost everything—and topped by a gallery of pilasters with Corinthian capitals. This imperial exit lends me a sense of well-being, amply nourished by the delicious chicken, cheese, bread, and wine. And so, with a bite of pear, I salute D980, my new course. Le Morvan has moved even closer to the road and looms on my left.

Had I followed the Arroux to its source, digressed just a little to the right on N81, I would have ended up at Dijon where M. F. K. Fisher and her beloved Al feasted some fifty years ago. The flavors of her essays fill me with a sweet sadness, for I had hoped to learn the taste of red Meursault, a Coq au Chambertin, with another also, but it was not to be. Once again, my transient nature has probably discouraged such companionship, but, in any event, I do not wish to dine alone in Dijon. So, I have taken the road to the left, D980, to enter the valley of the Ternin River and the rugged embrace of the Morvan.

Famous for its forests and rocky terrain, its Charolais cattle and network of rivers, this area was also known in the nineteenth century for the quality of its wet nurses. My Michelin tells me that leasing her breasts was "one of the most profitable occupations for the Morvan woman" and her milk was in great demand by the bourgeois mothers of Paris who thought it improper to nurse their own babies. Some local entrepreneurs carried their product to Paris while others stayed unbuttoned in their villages where little hungry mouths were brought to the local taps. Farmed out, as it were. Come to think of it, didn't Zola's *Nana* bring her unfortunate babe down here somewhere to be fed so as not to depreciate the charms of her own *nichons?*

So, it could be said, that I have put myself on a path between two gastronomical interests; to the right, the romantic and delicious tables of Dijon, and on my left, the rocky environs of more basic nourishment. But, let's put aside the literary allusion to Fisher, with its sigh of self-pity, because this footnote on the bountiful bosoms of Morvan has teased out another speculation. Perhaps I have taken this road as a metaphorical trip back to the tit that was abruptly popped from my mouth a half century ago. At least, as I drive this winding road, I take the opportunity to think about that rejection, to enjoy and even wallow in the anger I have lately begun to feel for that withdrawal of sustenance. Perhaps, I should examine the village women of Chissy, up the road, for a font at which I may slake my frustrated thirst? Too late, of course.

One of my friends says that I am a glutton, but my waistline has maintained a steady measurement of thirty-four for decades and most describe me as trim though stocky. Yet, in Pittsburgh I keep biscotti in one kitchen cannister and macaroons in another. The thought of skipping a meal, as my wife somtimes importunes, is a horror. Shifting the Ford's gears to negotiate the winding turns of D980, I play with the image of that baby mouth sucking in the empty air of Kansas City when my mother left me with her parents. Poor little hunger, never to be appeased—have I come all this way just to come upon this maudlin roadside epiphany?

For one thing, this unusual arrangement did put me on the road—maybe, even on this narrow route through the eastern part of the Morvan. From the age of two, I began to commute between Kansas City and New York; making the round trip almost every summer by train or Greyhound bus. Once on a Trans Western Airline's DC-3. On most of these trips, I traveled by myself in the care of a porter or a bus driver to be met by my mother or my grandparents at the terminus. So, I rolled back and forth through the eastern half of the U.S., coasting through towns and cities to take out a brief citizenship, or, for a few passing seconds, join a family in a car as they waited at a crossing. "A rolling stone gathers no moss," my mother was fond of saying and surely the credo seemed to work for her. Neither of us had read Sartre or Camus—neither Sartre or Camus had written much to read at that point. My mother would never read them. This French road has suddenly changed its number.

The route has become D20. The resinous perfume of conifers envelops my senses. Most of Paris's Christmas trees are cut from these plantations, another local product exported to the urban market. The valley has begun to close in on me and my Ford, and the road begins to ascend. I have to shift down. Flecks of brilliant sunlight begin to dart from the roadside vegetation to dash themselves against the windshield. The distance I have just traveled in the last few kilometers, to Kansas City and back and through decades and back, doesn't really surprise me. All memory, no matter the date of its manufacture, stays fresh and on the same shelf of the mind.

That particular weaning in Kansas City has probably given me a tramp's thirst for the unencumbered trek. For a period of more than ten years, I became an itinerant hack, driving from one campus to another to take up temporary appointments as a "visiting writer" (the title alone courts certain philosophical considerations). I told myself the purpose of this circuit riding was to relocate my identity, my self-esteem and to keep my children's respect. What lofty motives! But, maybe it was only the stone set rolling around within me, like a counterweight which propelled me away from home and a marriage, leaving behind my children and their affection though I may have sustained their respect. I put myself in transit—even on this road through the Morvan. Even in this essay.

But these gloomy thoughts are left below in the shadows of the river valley, for I come onto a high plateau in full sunlight as the road changes its number once again. D121. Here the pine forests are spotted with stands of ancient oak and beech, remnants of great forests that once stood here before they were logged and sent downriver to Paris for firewood. It is cooler as well as brighter, and Saulieu is just down the other side of this mesa. Midafternoon, but I have done quite enough traveling for one day, and I decide to stop there. Its kitchens have made the place famous.

The old Paris-Lyon post road runs through the town and has become the well-traveled N6; one of the principal routes through central France since the seventeenth century. In fact, the name of my hotel is Le Poste. Napoleon is supposed to have spent the night here on his way back from Elbe before going on to his appointment at Waterloo. The hotel is an attractive construction of exposed timbers and whitewashed stucco, and the corridor to my room falls way to the right and creaks underfoot like the passageway of a great ship under sail. My room is small but charming and with a window that looks out over the inner courtyard where horses must have been stabled and where I have parked my little blue Ford. But the dining room has been decorated with a belle époque elegance that puts me off, and the prices seem a little inflated as well. I crave a simpler atmosphere for dinner; the day has been complicated enough.

My journal does not record how I spent the rest of the afternoon. I don't recall visiting the famous basilica of Saint Andoche. I have no recollection of the local museum, which apparently features Saulieu's gastronomical history, nor did I pay my respects to the tomb of the animal sculptor Fracois Pompon. I will remember passing by his famous bull in a park near the road out of town the next morning. Perhaps, I took a nap.

Later, I choose the Lion d'Or from the several restaurants along the rue Grillot. The neat handscript of its menu, posted beside the entrance, pricks my appetite. The careful formation of the characters and the words' forthright demeanor on the page make for an appealing implication of the chef's manner in the kitchen. Also, the *prix fixe* is within my budget.

Inside the restaurant is quiet and almost bare of decoration. At several tables, diners are already meticulously at work and there is little conversation. This is a serious place. Seated, I become aware of the large glass panes, like the show windows of auto agency, that front the width of the dining room, and these have been closed to the traffic of the thoroughfare outside by oatmeal-colored drapes of a heavy material.

The woman who brought me to my table, returns with a menu, a basket of bread, and a small plate of *andouillettes* as a complimentary starter. She is obviously in charge, but her manner suggests that she may have just risen from one of the other tables, interrupted her own meal with a favored guest in order to serve me; yet, I am to take my time, not feel pressed by any consideration for her. Such distractions from her own pleasures come with her responsibilities to her patrons—to be assumed, m'sieur. She is dressed as if that afternoon she might have lectured somewhere on Descartes. She wears a tailored skirt and jacket, a straw-colored blouse of silk with an agate broach at the throat. Her shoes are expensive-looking, sturdy and polished. As I have been munching the crumbly saltiness of the little sausages, she has been waiting patiently for me to choose the wine.

When I look up from the menu, the expression on her face startles me. Madam has been worriedly observing me, concerned perhaps that I might come up with the wrong choice, that I would make a selection which would embarrass the whole dining room. Men would throw their napkins down in disgust, pushing back their chairs as their wives jump up trembling and affronted to push ahead of them children wailing and still clutching a half-eaten *tarte aux pommes*—all of them storming out of the place, arms raised and indignation spewing from their well-sauced lips.

I ask for the Cote de Beaune-Joliette. Madam brightens—her *"tres bien"* rings with approval. An economical choice, to be sure—but frugality is a virtue—and it is a vintage surely not unaware of its subtleties. Her attitude has so favored me, and the other diners have reasonably resumed their solemn degustations. I order the rest of my meal; a *soupe de lotte "Tante Angela,"* fricassee *canard au vinaigrette.* A mixed green salad.

It is only then that I notice the immense mural beside me. It takes up one half of the dining room's inside wall and depicts a chaotic scene: a carriage has just arrived at an inn—perhaps at Le Poste down the street where I stay. The artist is not primitive, but he has too faithfully reproduced every face and costume within this seventeenth-century context. Couples and relatives embrace and kiss. Children are lifted high and hugged. Dogs chase around the carriage's wheels and beneath the nervous hooves of horses reined in tight by grooms. Other boys hand down luggage from the coach. The innkeeper, his cheeks the size and color of crabapples, welcomes a stylish couple at the door. And in the center, like the star making her entrance, is a handsome woman who is attempting to manage her voluminous skirts as she steps down from the carriage. The artists have given her a rather roguish mien. This might be Madame Sévigné, who is remembered in Saulieu for getting a little tipsy during a stopover. Had she already had a few in the carriage, sipped from a small flask to settle the stomach on a bumpy post road, or does that expectant look reflect her anticipation of something agreeable to knock down in the tavern? Did she include this event in any of her famous letters to her daughter? *My dear Francoise—Your generous nature will perhaps embrace your mother's folly here in Saulieu for which I have given a statue in penance to the basilica of St. Andouche.*

Perhaps, I could write my daughter from Saulieu. Ask her to embrace my folly.

But the soup has been served. Aunt Angela's way with eels is fragrant with sage and saffron and maybe thyme. The dish resembles a tomatoless bouillabaisse and is thoroughly delicious. After Madame has circumspectly removed the empty bowl, I'm given a certain amount of time to contemplate what I have just enjoyed. The wine in my glass has rounded another mellow dimension. Then, she's back with the main dish which she presents with an offhand pride. The rich brown sauce, enforced by Armmagnac, glistens on the crackly surface of the duck leg adorned with sprightly green sprigs of watercress. The pungent meat pulls away from the bone like silk. Have the walnuts been added to the green salad especially to compliment the husky flavors of the canard or are they a usual flourish? The wine has darkened from ruby to garnet, deepening its flowing accompaniment to the meal like a subdued fanfare.

These accumulated satisfactions give me appetite to find something good in my daughter's letter. Whatever course this discord may take, she has, at least, confronted me, has strongly objected to my imperial imposition of self upon her own image. She demands self-definition and rejects my projection of who she is. How many women, I wonder, have been able to make such a stand but go through life in a continuous disagreement with men—and consequent dissatisfaction with themselves—because they never dissented with the original man in their lives? Our literature, our soap operas—the soap operas that pass for our literature—are driven by such melodramatic counterweights and the pattern becomes stuck in its own repetition. My mother never rebelled against her father's stern, sergeant-major manner, and then sought and found a similar Augustus in my father; only then, coming to her sense of self, to strike out on her own, refashioning herself but leaving me to do so, and that first distancing creating this lust I have for the solo trip—safety in solitude. And so on. For isn't this the ironic *casse en route,* that in recent years I have reinvented that initial abandonment by falling in love with young women who have yet to secure themselves and who must leave me to make their own images, find their own footing? Surely, this Cote de Beaune has properties Madame could never have imagined.

But there are important decisions to be made—should it be the *tarte aux poire* or *fromage?* She suggests, if only to close the stomach, a local cheese called Epoisses, and for reasons that would only greatly distress her, I am happy to place myself in her hands.

As if on cue, the bland consistency of music that has flowed through the restaurant from a discrete sound system has been strikingly interrupted. The indifferent envelopment of drapery and neat napery has been pushed aside by the crooning wail of a saxophone. It is a Toni Morrison saxophone, a tenor axe pulled down from the night sky and perhaps played by Stanley Turrentine to weave an American elegy of city nights, windows open on fire escapes as the loneliness of a lost love cools in its own sweat. I must be the only one in this room to hear this call; my fellow victualers continue their inexorable consumption. It's as if the soul, the jazz of America has searched me out, found me at this table in Saulieu to impose its sentimental reverie upon my wandering thoughts.

One face stands out in the mural, in fact he is looking just over my shoulder and meets my eye—the only figure to so engage the viewer. He is a village local, capped and booted, clay pipe in his mouth, and he has just returned from the hunt. He cradles a heavy fowling piece in one arm, a game bag hangs from one shoulder and he holds a large rabbit by the ears. It looks as if he has just rounded the corner of the inn to come upon this busy arrival scene, and he looks at me with a bemused expression. What's all this fuss about, he seems to ask? This human jostle is rather droll, don't you think?

I've seen this fellow before in Italy in frescoes of holy scenes—Old Testament barbarisms and awesome feats of levitation. Usually, the figure stands in the corner of the painting and sometimes bears the features of the painter—once or twice in the persona of an animal, a horse or a sheep. It is a device to call attention to what's going on but it does not ask for an interpretation, or impose an opinion, but only that we witness this human event. The hunter looking over my shoulder is saying, "See what's happening here. Here we all are." In transit, we pause for a little rest, step down from the day, careful of how we present ourselves, and have something to eat, a little wine, and perhaps write a letter or two at the end of this day in Burgundy.

1992

The Shape of the River

That the small orb of the eye encompasses all within this larger sphere and beyond strikes me as a miracle; like one of those fantastic toys Leonardo might have tricked together while pondering more ambitious engines of destruction or flight. In fact, Da Vinci did study the eye's design and his cold, mechanical drawings of it are of the same clinical quality as his diagrams of the human arm and leg. But, the sinews of vision are missing. Perhaps, they disappeared as the specimen cooled along with all the phantoms and colors that had exercised those delicate muscles; so, genius was left guessing—as we all are—as to how such a small vessel can hold so many images, so many shapes and sizes. The eye's ability to render color must have intrigued him as a painter as well, but how would he have responded to contemporary philosophical conceit that posits the eye manufactures color, that the world is actually a gray place until we humans look upon it? His ego might have warmed to the idea.

The eye of the memoirist also collects and holds a great variety of images within a small entity, sorting and giving them color to comprehend them. True, it is a backward sort of vision, but as it takes in the receding terrain, this sighting catalogs the important shapes and objects before they disappear over the horizon of the past, preserving them for future accounts and guidance. And just to throw in with Professor Whitehead for a moment, the whole lot is colored by the emotional acuity that the observer brings to the scene. It is this dynamic, this coloring in of the spaces within the lines, that must have stumped Leonardo and which makes one memoir more important than another, transforms a plain document of daily existence into a luminous testament of human experience. It is this spice of sensuality that gives a memoir lasting flavor.

When I think of great memoirs, three come to mind: Casanova's, U.S. Grant's, and Mark Twain's *Life on the Mississippi*. Three such disparate human beings never took up space in the same study, though Huck Finn's creator and the soldier-president do share a common corner in our history. Sam Clemens urged the penniless Grant, dying of throat cancer, to put down his memoirs, and then, the writer-turned-publisher raised a subscription to publish the result, which made Grant's widow and family wealthy.

In doing so, Clemens also secured the legacy of this amazing masterpiece for that part of the American bookshelf labeled "Memoir" and which, for some reason, is not a very large section though it has become a sort of catch-all in recent years. But what a story Grant's is! Talk about rags to riches and back to rags again—then riches once more. What a canvas Grant painted and what heroes and villains sat for their portrait! It's the stuff of a romantic thriller. Grant's humble origins, his lackluster attempts at business and his mediocre early army career (though his ability to ride any horse might foreshadow the later military successes). He was ridiculed and dismissed all along the way. But then came Vicksburg and then came the Wilderness and finally—Appomattox. Next came the White House but only to be betrayed by friends he trusted with his administration and whose dishonesty dishonored it. The most flamboyant Hollywood script cannot encompass the plot line of his life, the personae that peopled it, but within his own eye of memory he re-created the entire cast of characters, every battlefield and chamber—august or modest—to give that era breath and color. Moreover, contrary to the generals and statesmen whose autobiographies came after his, Grant wrote every word of the *Memoirs* himself while enduring the terrible pain of throat cancer every day that he sat down at his desk. The voice lost to the ravages of the disease magically surfaced in the prose his pen laboriously put down on paper.

That voice has a modest sound and a curiously sensitive tone for a great warrior to employ perhaps made raw by his own failures and embarrass-ments and the deadly claw in his throat. At the same time, no disingenuous note is struck; he was clearly aware of the history that had swirled around him and the part of that maelstrom that had been his doing. The prose is economical, what you might expect from a military mind, yet the right detail is simply supplied at just the right moment to bring a Lincoln or a Lee to life on the page. His insight into human personality is remarkable and possibly bears a kinship to what made him the awesome tactician on the battlefield that he was. And, as for those battles—they are all here too. Clearly presented, all the lines drawn and made understandable; every confrontation related with an underlying sadness, a terrible, unspoken cognizance that he had sent thousands to their death as he changed the nature of war forever. His grinding, relentless tactics stripped the hoary enterprise of its pomp and fatuous rituals, reducing it to the "hell" his subaltern, Sherman, described. Moreover, these chapters are tinted by his tragic awareness that he, U.S. Grant, had become the agent of an inexorable history that would extinguish a whole culture and a way of life for which, incidentally, he showed appreciation, and it is within the loss of this near mythical landscape that this sensual persona emerges, a man who enjoyed the flavors of alcohol and tobacco and the lift of a spirited horse between his legs.

From the formal parlors of Victorian America, it is a Pegasean leap to the ornate days and feverish nights of Jacques Casanova, but this self-advertised, all-time sensualist had a similar eye for detail. He registered the surrounding terrain with the same exactness, as did the former artilleryman from Illinois. The gaming tables, the carnal couches, the cells of a Venetian prison as well as the palaces beyond its walls are brought ripely to the eyes, ears, and even the nose of the reader. The interminable journeys back and forth over Alpine *cols* in hard sprung coaches are conveyed, jolt by jolt. The relief at wayside inns can be savored if not the heavy *daube* served at the communal table; for a gentleman always carried a private store of chocolate for such culinary emergencies to be shared privately with the intriguing madonna who has been bounced and jostled on the opposite tufted cushion.

I met this rogue in my father's library where I read him for all the "wrong" reasons, but were they so wrong after all? The pursuit and ravishment of duchesses, convent novices, and bar wenches are one with the rich tapestries, the corrupt liaisons of wealth and politics, the whole perfumed sourness of the eighteenth century that Casanova hung in my imagination— his amoral eye witnessed all of these happenings with equal fascination. I learned to read over the so-called scandalous episodes (their simple geometric solution of the same old problem quickly became monotonous) to get to a court scene, a view of Paris, or the demonstration of a mechanical robot that played a brilliant game of chess—one of the frauds he exposed—a construction hiding a midget grand master inside. He saw and reproduced the cold chambers of a usurer, the sounds of the Grand Canal at dawn, the trilling laughter of decadence in a palace corridor. He registered the sweat beneath the powder, the stench rising from the brocade and with a self-cutting wit, recorded the inanities of a period just coming to terms with comfort. He was a first-rate reporter, and the veracity of his accounts can be verified by the architecture he described such as La Fenice, the opera house completed a half dozen years before his death. Restored twice due to fires when I saw it in 1965, the artisans must have been guided by his account, for it looked to be the same extravaganza of gilded plaster pastry his aged eyes had caressed in 1792. A third catastrophe has taken the building again, and perhaps architects are currently turning the pages of his memoir once more.

As Grant visualized his time illuminated by the horror of a brutal civil war, Casanova looked beneath the faux finery of his period, and even his boastful, sexual escapades can be read as demonstrations of human hypocrisy—the often comic and usually useless efforts of a society attempting to corset its natural inclinations.

The same keen observation (a looking through the glass, if you will) is apparent in the young Sam Clemens as he learned to navigate the great river that divides our country. Sitting high in the wheelhouse of a steamboat, he heard the name of his alter ego for the first time —Mark Twain. He also took in the territory as no one before or after him has done, putting into our American souls a mythification of those muddy banks and bends in the river that can be argued perhaps but which is there, permanently. It is a trip downriver that writers and presidents, even whole sections of the population, have endeavored to navigate ever since. The shoals that disappear to appear elsewhere, the terrifying mist that can obscure a shoreline, backwaters festering and regenerating, boys fishing, small farms raising lazy smoke from a chimney, a villager waving—it's a picture produced with photographic realism and made indelible in our imaginations. As surely as those river banks fed their rich soil to the river, *Life on the Mississippi* put into our streams of unconsciousness chunks of nostalgia that enrich our American sensibility, though sometimes to a dangerously high level of spiritual cholesterol. But Clemens is aware of the hazards lying beneath this surface, as he looks back in this memoir of youthful exuberance and experience and saddened by what he knows is about to overwhelm this river basin, this view from the wheelhouse. Good pilot that he is, he issues a warning, "You have to know the shape of the river, if you're going to navigate her at night." It is a warning too many of our writers and politicians have ignored as they follow old charts. The irony must have occurred to the older Sam Clemens that he brought into print the memoirs of a man who, more than any other, destroyed the world which he himself re-created with such compelling reminiscence.

Grant, Casanova, and Clemens filtered their impressions through a sensual lens that is always variable and they must be taken in with the whole eye.

1994

In Montaigne's Tower

For Wayne Dodd

It is, as he writes, exactly sixteen "paces" across the thick paving stones of the circular floor. Three large windows are set into the curve of the stone wall to look out on the garden below and the landscape that falls away from this high butte on which the chateau was built. Greek and Latin inscriptions use the ceiling timbers of the room as a commonplace of collected wisdoms, but, of course, the bookshelves that Montaigne had carpenters fit into the stone radius of the outside wall are long gone and the beloved, well-thumbed volumes they kept put into a national archive.

It is Wednesday, the first of May; a sunny, cool morning that can almost be savored on the palate like the crisp, fruity Entre Deux Mer from the vineyards nearby. The city of Bordeaux, of which Montaigne was mayor in the 1580s, lies about fifty kilometers to the west. The chateau's caretaker is my casual guide, and he has continued to describe Montaigne's regimen in a manner that indulges my hobbled French. *Voici*—he walks to a far diameter of the room—is *le trou sanitaire* that the Master had masons open in the medieval wall—an innovative bit of sixteenth-century plumbing so that the calls of nature would only briefly interrupt the composition of an essay. On the opposite side of the chamber, another vent connects this tower study via an airshaft to the family chapel three floors below. Montaigne could remain scribbling at his desk and yet still hear the daily masses celebrated there.

My guide's right arm sweeps up and around in a wide windmill motion as he delivers what seems to be an often made but no less worn observation. His Gascogne expression is only slightly lifted. Yes, *je vois,* I nod; I get the idea: spiritual inspiration rises from below on one side to infuse the genius at his desk, and then the waste of this exchange is disposed through the opening opposite. He offers the procedure as a kind of basic model of creativity. *Aussi, c'est pratique!*

This pilgrimage made to my master's snug retreat has also been a journey to satiate once and for all, my appetite for France. Some of us may remember *les pommes frites* of the late 1940s. Plump slabs of potato sautéed in olive oil and shallots, sprinkled with parsley, that accompanied a *biftec* that was often *plus cheval que boeuf.* This cut of *frites* has all but disappeared, replaced by anonymously extruded perfections—deep fried and common to restaurants and road stands across the Republic. But, yesterday, I stopped for lunch at a Rouliers on the outskirts of Nicole on N113 to eat with truck drivers. Roast pork had been the *plat du jour,* and the tender slices of meat were accompanied by hand-cut chunks of potato sautéed crispy brown around the edges, redolent of garlic and sprinkled with chopped, fresh tarragon. Prefabricated spuds have yet to come to that part of the Lot-Garonne.

But I digress, for it is not only the food and wine that has mapped this ramble up from Provence and along the Garonne River. I have come to that time in my life when a return visit to a favorite place on earth will probably be my last view of it, my last taste of it. For instance, all the idling meanders I have made up and down the Meuse Valley, along the old battle lines of that horrible slaughter that shaped my century, have bred a melancholy passion for those fields of grain that indolently stretch out in the brilliant summer sun of Lorraine, beneath the dark green shoulders of the Argonne. The awful carnage that occurred there, its horrors muted by time, season my understanding of human idealism gone astray; remind me of how greed and stupidity can pollute the best intentions of men and women.

And here's another idea, surely preposterous in its vanity, but that in these places—this Dordogne Valley for instance where at certain turns of the road I encounter an earlier self—I might leave something of myself behind. Maybe, years from now in some of these villages the guise of my figure turning a corner will be confused by a resident with another. So, once again to digress, I seem to be talking now about memory, that two-way mirror we all carry of the past and before which we adjust our histories to fit the present. I don't recall that Montaigne ever specifically writes about memory, not even in any of his digressions, and this is curious for a man who so immersed himself in the bound volumes of antiquity. Perhaps, his time was so consumed by the present, by its current events—the Reformation with all its attendant barbarisms to cite just one—that the sixteenth century "now generation" found no space in their reflections for past events, for memory. His father, Pierre, was born only a couple of years after Columbus had discovered the New World, and that astounding happening was still making front-page news in Montaigne's day, stimulating him to write one of his better-known essays, "Of Cannibals."

So it is these memories of France, this glut of its past, that has partly driven me here to give homage to Montaigne, while satisfying once and for all this craving that almost amounts to a strange jealousy. It is no wonder that Montaigne and his contemporaries—like Shakespeare and Cervantes, or Copernicus and Galileo in science—were so brilliantly glib—they had brand new material to write about! To fly to the dead orb of the moon and return is an amazing feat but only that. On the other hand, to return with stories of an alter world populated with people much like us, who are going about their odd religions, raising zinnias and putting the Julian calendar into stone steps—now, that's the stuff of supermarket tabloids! Some inspiration! It is like the past catching up with the present to make an entirely different here and now. These days, it seems we mostly write of what might have been and our significant characters are all has-beens.

"I am overwhelmed by the past," Wright Morris will say to me. I am now on another pilgrimage, this one to California, and he has just met me at the door of his apartment in a retirement facility. Yet, when I follow him into the room, I am thinking of Montaigne's tower. The comic, complex intelligence that has so enriched our literature, and the understanding of our literature in his essays, is losing sight of its own perimeter to become almost as seamless as the inner wanderings and wonderings of his characters in such novels as *Field of Vision, Ceremony at Lonetree, Works of Love,* or *Love among the Cannibals*—to cite only some favorites from a huge bibliography. The astute focus on things, on moments that "tell all," effortlessly hones the conversation, but the *all* these things are supposed to tell has mysteriously eluded identification, fallen through the witty schema. A dry Nebraskan humor still edges the droll appraisal in the blue eyes; it is the look of a prairie-town barber who knows all about Pascal and Henry James, but isn't so sure his customers should hear about them. Just yet. "You see what is happening here," he will tell me with an uncanny objectivity. "This isn't what I expected."

It is as if time, that he had used so skillfully to arbiter his characters' inner lives, has lost the hands of its clock though the mechanism continues to function. Past and present are all one, real and unreal undivided. "I knew who you were, Hilary, when I came to the door, but which Hilary you were out of the pasts we shared, I did not know."

Last night I stayed in a small family hotel in the village of Branne. Montaigne's tower is only open to the public for a few hours once a week, on Wednesdays, and I have arrived on Tuesday, the last day of April. At the hotel de ville in Castillon de la Bataille, I was given directions to St. Michele de Montaigne, the tiny feudal hamlet established to serve the needs and security of the manor family. My Michelin tells me that Castillion received its distinctive title from a battle fought here in 1453 in which the English lost their control over this part of the Aquitaine, an early demonstration of the real being separated from the unreal which the British are still having problems learning today. But I digress.

My hotel is situated on the banks of the Dordogne River and at one corner of the village's covered market. In fact, when I open the window shutters in my room, I look directly out on the river which is fairly wide and fast-flowing at this point. Here, also, a modern steel truss bridge spans the crossing, probably a replacement of a stone bridge destroyed during one of the century's battles over the ownership of this territory. Almost due north from my window, at a distance of about eight kilometers, are the heights of St. Emilion, and I promise myself something from that domaine at dinner.

And it is a Chateau de l'Arrosse of the grand cru, rich in Merlot that Mme. Proprietaire decants for me in the hotel's plain dining room. About ten tables are placed correctly upon a gleaming wood floor, each with a small vase of blossoms, a kind of small lily, set precisely in the middle of the white paper table covers. Windows overlook the roof of an adjoining building and toward a slice of the river beyond. Two couples are already into their first courses as I taste the wine. They are of about the same advanced age, but one couple seems to be local citizens having a night out at the town's hotel. I had seen them earlier in the establishment's bar, having their aperitif, and they had been included in the familylike gossip—the give-and-take of the place. The second couple, seated near me and travelers like myself, speak a peculiar language that turns out to be Flemish.

"You speak French very well," the man says to me in heavy English. I had only ordered the eighty-franc menu from the timid young woman someone apparently has pushed out of the kitchen to take our orders. So, this compliment on my language skills puts me on guard. Am I being conned? I lightly tap the shape of my billfold within my jacket's breast pocket. But then, I put them together with the large Mercedes that is parked next to my little Peugeot in the market square. In addition, the authority of the man's polished baldness suggests respectability. They are, in fact, art dealers returning from a business trip in Spain to Belgium.

My duck is crisp and tasty and served with a pureed medallion of something that could be turnip and its musty root flavor plays off well against the sweet pungency of the fowl. Mme. Proprietaire has brought her young son, a boy of about three or four, into the dining room to greet the guests. The child, guided by his mother, makes a solemn tour of our three tables, offering his hand with a large-eyed frankness. I met his father in the lounge before dinner, just as the man returned from his daytime job. He had put his lunch pail down next to the bar sink, rolled up his sleeves and took up the gossip and the servicing of the locals as his wife left to attend kitchen matters. The art dealers have been trying to engage me in conversation, mostly their complaints on the state of contemporary painting. They say that all worthwhile work has already been collected. My mind is elsewhere, and has no place for their dilemma.

Montaigne's tower was closed today, but I had been able to visit the ancient, small church of St. Michele in the writer's village. A local resident had shown me the crypt behind the altar where the writer's heart had been buried. Whether at his behest or by his widow's sympathetic direction, I do not know, but his heart was placed alongside the remains of his father in September of 1592. The rest of him was entombed in a cathedral in Bordeaux only to be moved about in the next several centuries in a ludicrous pawn game run by prefects, archbishops, and academicians. But his heart remains next to his father in his home village.

We know something about that relationship. A robust seigneur of the Renaissance, the elder Montaigne trained servants to wake his baby son to the strains of harp and flute. Moreover, all the help who served the young child spoke only Latin to him and he to them; he heard no French until his fifth or sixth year. Pierre Montaigne, something of an early environmentalist, introduced his son to animal husbandry and a respect for all animals, for the miracles of plant life and the cultivation of the vineyard and granary. The arts of war were not neglected, and his father showed him the handling of weapons and armor, for the young noble would need this expertise if he were to serve his king and protect his estate. In this last curriculum, horsemanship was the important course of instruction, and under his father's tutelage, the two of them often riding side-by-side into Bordeaux, Montaigne learned a lifelong appreciation for horses, a pleasure in the power and movement of a good horse under him even when enduring the awful agony of kidney stones that attacked him late in life. He writes that the inspiration for many of his essays came to him on the back of a horse, contrary to the theory to be suggested by my guide at the tower. "We can't afford to take the horse out of his essays," Emerson was to write centuries later.

I read of this companionship, so intimate and resolute even in death, with a mixture of wonder and envy. My own father, separated from me in life as well as death, lies in a small village of Petersburg in central Illinois— his "heart's home," he called it. No part of me will ever join him in that rural graveyard for our destinies have put us on divergent paths; yet, he did pass on to me some important lessons. Not in horsemanship, for sure. No Latin and less Greek, but an affection for the ideas and literature born in those languages. A love of music, though I have not his heavy taste for such composers as Brahms and Dvorak. My skepticism of certain human endeavors and pretenses—such as altruism—is a reflection of his thinking. But books, keeping a library. There's the connection.

To my wife's agitation, books are piled on our tables, spill in heaps from stuffed shelves, and lie about the floor and on chairs like spoiled pets. I have a miser's greed for books, and I pick them up at random to read a passage or follow an argument, inhabit a poem. I carry them from room to room, portable transitions of thought, of the past into the present, only to put them down in a maddening disorder. Guests sometimes ask, "Have you read all these books?" My answer must be, no. But they are there for me to read, or reread, some day. If I am to have wealth it is in my books and when I regard their spines pressed together on the bookshelves, observe the casual sculptures they make on a table, my spirit becomes cozily furnished.

My father's love of books can be measured by the depth of his anguish caused by the loss of his library in the course of his first marriage's divorce. In all of our meetings, my visits to him in New York City, the loss of that library invariably entered his conversation. By then, of course, he had collected other volumes of Homer, Goethe, Keats and company, but these were reproductions, so to speak, and did not carry the imprint of that first handling, the scent of that first enthusiasm. Over the years, he would write the son of that marriage pleading with him to find some way to return the books of his library to him, but the son always claimed vague difficulties; he could do nothing. After my father's death, the son revealed he had had the library all along and, in fact, he donated the library to a collection and took it off his taxes.

So, in this modest dining room of this small hotel in Branne, I have been taking account of these quite different relationships between fathers and sons; one so ardently physical, using Aristotle's empirical methods to learn of the world, and the other distant, cooly intellectual and seeking worldliness in books. It must be evident that I have nearly consumed the St. Emilion, for, together with the silky surfeit of a creme brulée, my senses have become transported, reality addled and sentimentality ascends. I yearn to fit myself beneath that bony cheek in Illinois.

"All the Rembrandts in the Hermitage are fake," the art dealer says. The Belgium couple finish their coffee and leave.

This morning, their big, gray Mercedes has gone when I throw my bag into the Peugeot and drive across the Dordogne to retrace the twenty kilometers east toward St. Michel de Montaigne. The tower, and its companion at the opposite end of a stone rampart, are all that is left of the chateau that Montaigne knew. The main building was destroyed by fire and rebuilt along the same lines in 1885. However, the portal is the same one Montaigne had used, and the family chapel on the ground floor of the tower was unharmed. A mural on the wall behind the small altar shows St. Michel subduing a dragon within the lion paws of the family crest. A fresco trompe d'oeil around the walls attempts to suggest a larger diameter for this cell.

The second floor contains a bedroom where Montaigne often spent the night, too weary from creating this new form of literature to cross the courtyard to the family chambers. Even what we call the genre was his invention from the French verb *essayer*—to try, to test. Then, the top floor, this large circular garret with a much smaller alcove with a fireplace. Winter quarters for the essayist. On one wall of this room, he had painted the declaration of his retirement on his thirty-eighth birthday; "long weary of the servitude of the court and public employments, while still entire . . . to the bosom of the learned Virgins." That is, the Muses. The tower is thereby consecrated to "his freedom, tranquility and leisure."

Following my guide up the narrow corkscrew stairs to this top floor, it's amused me to fit my feet into the same worn hollows of the stone treads that Montaigne must have trod; the apprentice footfalls literally following in the master's steps. But the attic where genius labored is a barren place. The textures of the thousand books, by his count, that once lined the room and which may have softened its hard ambiance, are missing and the place looks like a prison, a dungeon with windows. At the age of thirty-eight, Montaigne voluntarily exiled himself from family and friends; put himself in this stone tower to serve the Muses, the cruelest and most demanding of wardens. Sometimes either Henry III or Henry of Navarre would call him out for shuttle diplomacy between their warring thrones, or a turn at the Bordeaux mayoralty would be forced upon him, but this is where he spent most of his remaining twenty-one years. It's tempting to think that all those books gave him the freedom to travel through these walls, through space and time, but I've never been entirely convinced of the idea that the act of creation, of choice, grants freedom. Moreover, if freedom is to be gained, it is usually at the expense of others.

Yet, in this bastille, the human mind was liberated to discover itself, and this amazing mind put together the means for that discovery. "What do I know?" he penned one morning at his desk and the question stimulated 103 essays in answer. The domain of human sensibility was enlarged as Columbus's elementary navigation had enlarged the external world.

" . . . but I am no longer so sanguine, being less certain than I once was as to what it is to be human," wrote Wright Morris in an essay on photography, "The Camera Eye." And it is curious that this major American novelist, so inventive of character in his pages, focused on only one human figure as a photographer—the famous back of "Uncle Harry" entering a barn door. His photographs picture the things and objects people have used; combs and chairs and implements as well as the rooms and barbershops and dining rooms they have passed through—just left maybe. These subjects of his photographs are sympathetic companions to his fiction. Tangible possessions are transformed by Morris's wordless camera into emblems of the men and women who may have owned them, where as the actual people could only be "captured" on the high-speed emulsion of his language. Words on paper made the real picture.

Perhaps what we mistakenly call reality is only the subject that has held still long enough to be photographed. The energies and multi-layered qualities of human ambition are never at rest and move too fast for ordinary film. They can only be "taken" by the novelist, the poet, or the playwright. Recent attempts to transfer to movies the wordy musings on the human condition by Wharton, James, and Conrad have resulted in earnest, entertaining failures. And we must accept the filmmakers' defense that movies are a different medium. They are. They are only composed of pictures, but are they as real as they should be? Really real?

Perhaps, Montaigne's claim that he was the only subject of his essays was made once too often to believe its humility; however, looking into himself, he captured an authentic picture of his world and its citizens. Mulling through the volumes that once lined these walls, he recovered his world's past in order to reproduce its present. I stand in this cool, stone cell where these translations took place and still feel their heat. I think of the albums of photographs that supposedly represent our time. Go to your local used magazine store, and flip through the piles of old *Life* magazines, see *Life* going to the party that was this XX century. But they won't give you the whole picture. Only the camera of the mind can produce images adequate to the authors of the time.

"Look at that," Wright Morris will say to me in California. On the floor beside his easy chair is a large, coffee-table format book of photographs— the planet earth taken from space, from the moon. The cover shows a blue disc scarfed in the wispy egg whites of clouds, and not a sign of life. "It doesn't look like anything," he will say.

1996

Son of Spoon River

The photographer from *Newsweek* has walked me around to the rear of St. Pat's and to a corner in the gothic masonry where the light is even. He has pulled a light meter out of his kit and holds it before my face.

"A Luna-Pro," I say. "I just got one myself."

"Oh, yeah? You a photographer too?" He's begun shooting me with a heavy, black Nikon. The camera's film advance whirs disinterestedly, and I believe any subject, breathing or still, would excite its sensitive mechanism. Even the author of a newly published family biography.

"Yes, I do some," I have answered. I was about to give him a short résumé; my time as a naval correspondent, using the old Kodak Medalist; the two or three shows I have mounted in pizza joints and basement galleries; the calendar shots I have sold to a stock agency. But his casual proficiency, his expertise with his equipment, makes me shy to suggest a collegiality.

Just last month, in a hubristic rush, I traded in my old Weston exposure meter, a reliable tool in my photo kit for many years, for one of these same nine-volt Gossens whose complex computations have made the mystery of illumination for me even darker. On the other hand, this new meter has revealed the deception my old Weston has played upon me all the years as I've held it up to subjects; allowing me to think its measurements of reflected light were simple factors rather than the complicated theories of phenomena that the Luna-Pro posits again and again. To be sure, the selenium photocell of the Weston had transposed available light into equations of shutter speeds and lens stops that had given me perfect exposures every time, but, clearly, the process has been too easy—incomprehensibly correct if not accidentally accurate. When I offered the Weston as part of a trade on the Luna-Pro, the owner of the photo shop was amused by its antique naïveté and finally, as a favor, took it off my hands.

This ambition to make more accurate photographs of a subject can inspire a lust for more and more equipment, the most advanced gadgetry, because once the shutter is clicked, the image registered becomes permanent. In that instant, the subject has been taken for all time, so the picture ought to be "perfect." This freeze of reality is perhaps the dubious achievement of photography and makes for a curious cannibalism of subject matter. For example, the monumental clay bulk of the St. Francis Church in Rachos de Taos, New Mexico, has been printed indelibly in our minds by Ansel Adams's photograph of its back wall, the eloquent play of shadow and light along the curve of its adobe buttress. No other photographer, professional or amateur, has been able to take that church from a different angle, many have tried and most end up with a photograph very similar to the one Adams made in 1929. He made *the* picture of it.

So, it comes down to who first holds the camera, puts the angle held on the object—the "third eye," as Cocteau observed about the relationship between camera and photographer. The ingenious mechanics that function between this eye and its object merely convey and compute the glance; then, makes the image permanent. Similarly, another kind of mechanical focus, no less automatic, is sometimes turned upon an individual which measures only the surface reflection to make a quick study; then, this angle is printed to make the picture instantly archival and nearly impossible to revise.

"You know what they are calling you at the office?" The *Newsweek* photographer is packing up his gear. My image has been fixed on the film of his Nikon. "They call you, 'Son of Spoon River.' "

My reason for writing the book that has caused this photo session was to put down on paper for my children some of the stories my grandfather had told me—the history of his immigration to this country from Ireland and his adventures toward a citizenship never fully granted within the cruel freedom of America.

But to write about Tom Coyne, I would have to write about my grandmother, and to write about my grandparents, I would have to write about their daughter who had left me with them, at the age of one year, to be raised in Kansas City, Missouri. And to write about my mother, I would have to write about my father, Edgar Lee Masters.

The father, then, is only one of the four characters in this family biography, and he is by no means the most important to the narrative—as he was not to my life. Moreover, during the course of the book's composition, the figure of the mother forged a commanding presence in the text as she had done in all of our lives. However, my father *was* this lawyer-turned-poet who published a book of poems in 1915 that turned the American literary establishment on its head, thereby acquiring a fame that had not been foreseen and a success probably never to be forgiven by some.

At the same time, to say that his importance in this work was secondary is to shuffle over the hole card I must have hoped to play in this game of chance called *publishing*. However small his part in the drama might be, it seemed to me his appearance in it might attract some interest in the manuscript. But, this didn't happen. My agent refused to offer it, and I circulated the manuscript, mostly on my own, for three years and to every major publishing house, some more than once, until David Godine of Boston finally published it, in 1982, under the title *Last Stands: Notes from Memory*.

True, it is a difficult book to categorize—always a necessity for the marketing minds of publishing. Was it a biography or a memoir—a novelized autobiography? Also, its narrative was said to be too eccentric, not the usual sequential plotting and with jarring juxtapositions of time and place, startling shifts forward and backward. The wise-heads at Houghton-Mifflin, Macmillan, Farrar, Straus and Giroux, Doubleday, Knopf, and on down the line didn't like it. Once published, the same "problems" they had with the manuscript were lavishly praised, even imitated, and the book has been called an "American classic."

But perhaps those editors had been influenced by the portrait of Edgar Lee Masters hanging in their minds—the picture of a "one-book author" whose damnable luck had exceeded his commonplace gifts, and for whom room was never to be made on William Blake's mountain. And here comes the son, they may have said, daring to put words on paper that allude to this embarrassing figure in American literature. Maybe I should have left the father out of the book altogether? Could I have written the memoir under a pseudonym?

A farmer's son inherits the farm and his husbandry will be evaluated by the jury down at the Grange, comparisons will be drawn between his and his father's management. But, that he decided to take up agriculture is almost never held against the son. A similar tolerance is extended in other lines of work; coal mining and steel wrangling; the law and medicine, even insurance. High-wire acts. Parent and child working at the same task; weaving straw hats, taking up arms or turning pots—it's an old custom. But in the arts, and especially literature, a peculiar filter puts a harsh vignette around the child who dares to follow a parent into the business of putting ideas and emotions into words on paper. Often, the offspring's work is seen from this angle—his or her modest attempt sometimes found insulting to a critic by its very attempt. And it is true, some of us have struck foolish postures before the camera, have made ourselves into curios by dropping the name of a parent to advance our own scribbling. But is this a class picture?

Like all first novelists, I had no say in the biographical material printed on the cover flaps of *The Common Pasture* by Macmillan in 1967. Since then, I've been able to keep my father's name off of subsequent book covers and out of publisher's press releases—save for *Last Stands*. After all, he is a character in the story. But as my virtue frustrated publicists, surely I had to admit the relationship had already been established with the publication of that first novel. The late Granville Hicks reviewed this book as one of "Nine Bright Beginnings" in the *Saturday Review of Literature*. His complimentary notice singled out the book's compact structure and the style while he identified me as "the son of Edgar Lee Masters who takes as dark a view of human nature as his father."

Now, every writer carries in his kit bag a packet of instant insecurity that can be transformed by an innocuous comment, or even a casual observation, into a draught of toxic Kool-Aid. Just to reproduce a clear and faithful image of human experience is, almost by definition, impossible (read Mary Shelley), and to even attempt this feat is to raise an insolence that courts eternal punishment. If nothing else, it makes for a chronic case of the jitters. But add to this common doubt, the thought that one's work may be scolded or praised because of a single roll in a bed, way in the past, and the ingredients for a stew of paranoia are in the pot.

Some thirty years later, I still wonder if that decent, little novel was put into that honored circle of first novelists because Granville Hicks, as literary historian and critic, was amused by its author's parentage. If I have felt that this might have been so—that a special privilege had been extended—surely, the idea must have occurred to others. Let me shoot this from another angle. What if Robert Stone, another one of those "nine bright beginnings" on Hicks's list, had been born of a famous writer—would his fiction be valued any more or any less for it?

Dissatisfaction with one's faux celebrity might have something to do with who happens to be next to you when the shutter clicks. We should be careful of whom we stand near during these moments of record—class reunions, family picnics. Who wants to be fixed for all time, shoulder to shoulder with the classmate who helped Nixon fix the Constitution or with Uncle Jack, the jolly embezzler? But sometimes we are not given the chance to choose our place; we are arranged alphabetically, if you will. So perhaps my complaint is that my father *was* Edgar Lee Masters, the one-shot author from Chicago. If his name had been Cheever or Van Doren or Hemingway or Updike, would I be taking these coy pains with the reader to establish a little distance between him and me? I hope that I would be.

What if our name had been Dumas?

As young Alexander was getting into print, *le pere* wrote him, "You shouldn't sign your name Dumas. My name's too well known, and I can't really add *the Elder.* I'm too young for that!" But this colossus of French literature (Michelet called him "one of the forces of nature") was clearly a very hard act to follow. He authored over three hundred novels, hundreds of plays, many of which he had adapted from his own novels, such as *The Count of Monte Christo,* or wrote his own versions of *Hamlet* and *Macbeth.* The senior Dumas offered to collaborate when young Alexander expressed an interest in writing, but the son turned down the offer. Even so, when Junior published *Camille* in 1848, at the age of twenty-four, salon gossip whispered that the father had written the novel for him. After all, it was known that father and son shared a mistress or two so why not a plot; especially one that concerned a consumptive courtesan, modeled on an actual woman they both might have bedded? However, the delight with which Paris embraced the appearance of this son following his father overwhelmed such calumny. When the novel became the play *La Dame aux Camellias* and later, with Verdi's help, the opera *La Traviata,* Dumas *fils* had named his own path. "My best work, dear boy," his father wrote him, "is you."

The photograph we have of Alexander Dumas, Jr., shows him lounging in a chair, heavy-lidded and with a comfortable girth about him that projects his success. But as that photographer counted off the seconds it took to fix this image on the gummed paper plate, did he think to himself, "This is the Son of Monte Christo?" Surely, he did not raise the question with the author of *La Dame aux Camellias.*

Virginia Woolf has ably documented the fate of Shakespeare's sister, but she has ignored—for reasons we can only guess at—the playwright's son, the one that survived him. Brother to Hamnet and named from his grandfather, John Shakespeare made a number of appearances as a boy in his father's early plays—assorted babes in arms and pages. When he landed the role of Beatrice in *Much Ado About Nothing,* tongues must have wagged. No account has been found of his performance but all must have agreed that he cost the company little. Two years later, the plum of Ophelia in *Hamlet* was denied him because his voice had changed—a kind of leveling by the gods that probably gratified the ale klatch down at the Mermaid. So, with or without his father's influence, John's performing days were over. Apparently, he didn't have the mind to do tragedy.

Meanwhile, he had been scribbling little scenes of his own—mostly improvisations and fantastical stuff involving bears and nymphs. Some of these were played out during the intervals of his father's tragedies as the audience bought oranges and milled about. His name has never been attached to these interludes—those that survive—probably because his father was already having trouble with Francis Bacon who had been bankrolling some of the productions and was even pressing him to have his own name put on some of the plays. Considering all that, the charge of nepotism was something father William surely did not want to deal with. "My name is too well known here in London for you to prosper und'it," the Bard probably wrote his son. "By any other name, your work will be the same."

One source indicates that in 1610 a fringe company in Hempstead produced a play by a certain John Brokespear that was said to be based on a recent essay by Montaigne—all about cannibalism in the New World. The play's dark view of human nature may have seemed familiar to some in that suburban audience, and it is even likely that the senior Shakespeare attended opening night, because *The Tempest* appeared the following year. Backstage, during the cast party, father threw arms around son's neck. "Dear boy," he might have said, "you have given me my best work."

The son's play has been lost, perhaps another reason Mrs. Woolf never mentions him, nor did Ben Jonson refer to it in any of his journals, no doubt to save his good friend, Will, further embarrassment. Evidently, Junior went back to Stratford and got into real estate, subsequently to be joined by his father who had burned out after thirty-eight plays— a couple of which he needed John Fletcher to finish. Curiously, this ironic twist has escaped mention in even the most scrupulous biography of the Avon master.

So, it can go both ways.

Halfway through high school, it dawned on me that my father was a person of some importance, but from the beginning, this importance was oddly marred. The work on which his fame rested was faulted by some and dismissed by others. A lucky hit. If *Spoon River Anthology* was granted a place in literature at all, that place would be qualified by some as being accidentally won, like the lottery; therefore, unearned. His sudden, unaccountable promotion in 1915 from a lawyer-poetaster, hardly known to Harriet Monroe's *Poetry* bunch, into a front-rank literary figure raised the mean jealousy of a Sandburg and engendered the undying competitive hatred of a Frost.

Certainly, *Spoon River* stands far above the rest of his work, some fifty or more published novels, books of poetry, and plays, but so does it stand high in the American anthology as well. The metaphorical village he raised on the banks of an Illinois river can even be located on the maps of Poland or Korea or Brazil—pick almost any plate in the atlas—and the dramatized aspirations and confusions of its citizenry are a permanent part of the human comedy. That Masters had somehow put this masterpiece together stretched the credulity of the salon wisdom—and still does. It should not have happened to him. Let's see him do it again, the cry went up!

I've always been struck by the similarity between the machine politics I observed my grandmother manipulate as a worker for the Pendergast organization in Kansas City and the kind of associations and trade-offs that occur in what is sometimes called "po-biz." You-do-for-me-and-I-do-for-you is standard operating procedure for both institutions, and, the figure of an independent is regarded with suspicion in both of these precincts. An individual who has nothing to trade and no outstanding IOUs is never completely accepted by either and certainly never trusted.

So, probably my father's feelings were hurt. He had expected to be received into that legislature that Shelley had talked about, but, instead, he found a membership not much different in kind from what the ward heelers of Chicago politics oversaw. Here, he thought, he had produced this volume of poems which a lot of people thought were kind of special; yet, far from accepting him, the Sandburgs, the Frosts, the Untermeyers, and the Van Dorens immediately questioned his credentials. He had only one outstanding IOU, to William Marion Reedy who had originally published the poems in his *Mirror,* and though he might have offered free legal advice— and often did—he had no literary favors to trade with any of his new peers. Also, his prairie boy's enthusiasm for the classics must have bored hell out of them.

On occasion, I would hear him mutter a defense to this charge of being a one-book author, calling up such witnesses as Cervantes and Chaucer, Boccaccio and Whitman. No doubt, the commercial success of *Spoon River Anthology,* as much as its critical acclaim also contributed to him being put on a different set of scales. So, he became bitter, and, for some, this reaction was further confirmation of his smallness. He was caught in a bad light and couldn't turn away.

Today's popular entertainment of celebrity-bashing, similar to the bear-baiting of early times, is a way to punish an individual or a group that does not enforce the image our society has of itself, the way it wants to appear. The idea is to distort the camera angle or paste up a picture of these outsiders and offenders that presents a profile that will deserve the establishment's scorn and ridicule. An archival image. The technique is the

staple of supermarket tabloids, but to come across the same design in more
worthy journals, comes as a shock.

Recently, Elizabeth Hardwick had a merry time with my father's history
in the *New York Review of Books.* In an essay, ostensibly a review of a new
biography of Vachel Lindsay, Ms. Hardwick presented a picture of my father's
last half dozen years and death that resembled the farcical helter-skelter of a
scene by Feydeau—how my mother supposedly pulled him this way and that,
across one state line and another—to fabricate a rather ludicrous picture
of a period in their lives. While economically stringent, their last years
together were actually very serene and comfortable, and my father died
in a dignified circumstance not all poets have enjoyed. Hardwick had the
chronology wrong, the states wrong, the dates wrong, the circumstances
wrong, and the whole package delivered with the saucy verve of the *National
Enquirer.*

But was this only sloppy research? Surely, Ms. Hardwick was not unaware
of the pitfalls and uncertainties of a poet's life in America, so her pasteup of
my parent's history is a little puzzling. Could her distortions have been
a reflection of that first picture of my father's life and work that the
establishment took back in 1915? The editors of the *Review* printed my
corrections, and Ms. Hardwick, in a somewhat pouty response, admitted
to most of her errors and omissions.

But, one last exposure and this one from an architectural angle, if you will.
Like Adams's church in New Mexico. On the red sandstone facade of the
Hotel Chelsea in New York City are plaques commemorating the different
tenancies in this old hostel of various poets, writers and composers; all
are worthy to be so noted. From 1930 until 1944—fourteen years—Edgar
Lee Masters lived and worked in rooms on the second floor of the Hotel
Chelsea, but his name does not appear on this quaint poets' cornice on West
23rd Street. Not on Blake's mountain—nor even on this pile of rock.

1995

Three Places in Ohio

A little more than midway through my journey, I prepare to descend from the twentieth floor of Pittsburgh's sparkling Gateway Center where I have just met with a lawyer to make my last will and testament. The elegant offices of his firm offer a comfort so deeply carpeted as to soothe the most anxious footfall, so I enter the elevator confident that my last good intentions are in good hands. Just as the elevator doors slide close, another man slips through.

He appears to be a senior partner. Well-tailored and at ease with himself, he looks at me sideways and smiles. "What are you doing for the Fourth?" he asks as we begin to descend.

Well, as a matter of fact, my wife's birthday falls a few days after the holiday—and on a weekend this year—and I have planned a little excursion, a surprise trip to East Liverpool, Ohio, about an hour's drive from Pittsburgh; just across the Ohio River.

"It's only part of the festivities," I hasten to tell him, "but there's a small café there, Brickers, where we had a marvelous breakfast a few years ago. Grits and ham gravy, wonderful home fries, eggs fried in butter and biscuits. Strong coffee. Like an old-time place." My companion has been nodding knowingly. Despite his cosmopolitan manner and attire, he is clearly a man of solid tastes.

"Then you should drive south from there," he tells me as we near the ground floor. "Take Route 7 along the river to a small place called Fly. There's a restaurant there on the riverbank that serves wonderful pie." The doors open smoothly, and he disappears into the milling lobby.

So, go to Fly for pie. It must be a message sent me from some divinity on high, from at least the twentieth floor, and I am particularly receptive to such oracular recommendations since for the past hour the subject on the stylish conference table upstairs has been my death. Nor is this the first time I have visited these legal chambers under the threat of death.

A few years ago, an associate began to make abusive phone calls to me and in one of these he even threatened to kill me. Surely, his behavior is an extreme example of the puny power struggle familiar to all institutions, but

I took him seriously; moreover, the man's maniacal jealousy began to affect my home life. My wife heard one of his messages on our answering machine and was unable to sleep that night. So, I took my complaints, along with one of these phone messages my wannabe assassin obligingly left behind on tape, to a lawyer of this firm. He took the attacks seriously too, for they constituted, according to him, "harassment with the intention to cause emotional harm," a statute upheld by the Supreme Court, and he notified my assailant of this finding, adding that legal action would be taken if he continued this maliciousness.

The lawyer's letter has not quelled the man's vicious anger, enwrapped in a sanctimonious manner so finely made as to suggest he waits to fill a vacancy in the Holy Trinity—as Mark Twain would observe—but I have been able to answer the phone without anticipating his malevolent harangue.

But every itinerary includes a death threat, and we must learn to live with the knowledge of this stopover, even to devise strategies to give some dimension to its immeasurable closure. And what better strategy on this bright July weekend but to go to East Liverpool, Ohio, and to Brickers Cafeteria and Deli for a late breakfast.

East Liverpool is a small city of about fourteen thousand people that has come to be known as the "pottery capital of the world." Soon after the area was surveyed as part of the Northwest Territory, the local soil was discovered to be rich in a clay that made high-quality ceramic products. By the end of the nineteenth century, a thriving industry turned out tableware and other china articles, and the amount of money made from clay pots can be estimated from the elaborate facades of Victorian mansions that line the side streets of East Liverpool today. Several companies continue the trade, including the ubiquitous Fiestaware, and the same natural resource supports other firms that make clay products for the electronic and communication industries.

In 1934, the little town on the Ohio River achieved a momentary national notoriety when the rural hoodlum "Pretty Boy" Floyd was gunned down by G-men in a nearby cornfield. His bullet-ridden body was put on display in a local funeral home to attract thousands of Depression-era mourners who stood in long lines to pay tribute to this hero who had dared attack the banks that had ruined them. For some reason, as I write these words, a picture forms in my mind of J. Edgar Hoover, clutching a Thomson submachine gun to his immaculate pin-stripe and wearing a grim look and a snap brim fedora. I wonder if he had been in that cornfield.

But it is Brickers Cafeteria and Deli ("Home-Cooked Food") that brings us to East Liverpool this morning, and to pass into its aroma is to enter a realm of orderly satisfactions. Of life. The delicatessen is in the front of the establishment and it is not particularly unique. But at the rear and slightly to the right lies the grill and small cafeteria, and here motherly and even grandmotherly women wearing crisp blue smocks over their dresses cook and serve the delicacies that make this unpretentious place one of the more noteworthy culinary haunts along the Ohio River.

At the grill, a customer may order eggs in any form, pancakes. Grits, corn beef hash gravies from red-eye up through the more subtle whites, side orders of various meats, including homemade sausage, and of course— home fries. The home fries have been neatly pushed to the back of the cook top so that their innate goodness is slowly teased to the surface by the continuous heat. These are not the mechanically cut spuds found on the usual grill and whose conformity of size and shape discourages the palate even before the first forkful. The home fries at Brickers are a tumbled, jolly pile of tubers, chopped indiscriminately into a countless profusion of shapes and sizes. The smaller nuggets have been basted in bacon grease to a charred crunchiness that when taken in the mouth with a larger, more pliant portion can flood the darkest introspection with undeniable light. "Death is not present here," Epicurus might say, "so it should not concern us."

The lady at the grill turns pancakes in one corner of the surface and rolls sausages over in another section. Two eggs cook sunny side in a third area. "So her water broke this morning," she tells a colleague who holds plates of steaming grits, "and I said to him what did the doctor say, and he says any time today. Oh, I have to go through that again." Kathleen has tarried at this station, transfixed by the possibilities sizzling before her, while I move on to the small cafeteria-style tray railing. It is only about six feet long and passes before a case stocked with freshly baked muffins, sticky buns, pies, mad popovers. I am trying to be a man of restraint, the secrets and the delights that wait us downriver in Fly abetting my self-control. But then, a hand-scrawled card on the counter announces the morning special to be sausage gravy on biscuit. I must have it.

I know something about gravy and what makes good gravy. I was once married to a woman from West Virginia who is probably one of the great gravy makers of all time. Moreover my grandmother's Sunday gravy from roast chicken drippings yet pools in my memory in all its brown luxuriance. My old friend Bill Humphrey often bragged of the gravy cooked up in his East Texas childhood, and so it seems to me that the great gravies in the American cuisine all have been stirred on southern stove tops. "Poor folk food," Bill used to say appreciatively as his wife Dorothy blended the mixture over a moderate flame with the same patient respect she gave to risotto or polenta—two supreme concoctions incidentally that share similar humble origins.

To be ignorant of gravy and its making is to be ignorant of the basic ingredients of life and how to appreciate that life. Flour and grease, some water and a little flavoring—these ordinary elements when combined rightly produce an extraordinary nostrum that can appease almost any human hunger, alleviate almost any anxiety. Almost.

We have been waiting for our orders as we sip coffee ("55 cents—15 cents refills") in one of the plain, plastic-covered booths in the dining area. Behind us, in several booths near the exit, is a small legislature of older men, the shadow government to be found in small towns like East Liverpool. They drink coffee and smoke and talk and then drink more coffee—a regular rotation to and from the coffee urn at the cashiers which probably explains the charge for refills.

But our dishes have been served by another one of the women in a blue smock, and I wonder if they may belong to some sort of local guild, perhaps some older and wiser society of Vestals sworn to minister to homely needs. Kathleen looks past her selection of eggs, bacon, home fries, and toast to my rather bland-looking plate of sausage gravy and biscuit. How deceptive the prosaic can be in nature and human affairs; how it can disguise a host of eccentricities, evil motivations, and so it is with sausage gravy. But I'm not about to bring up this reflection for she is already engaged with her breakfast. And so am I.

The moment my fork cuts through the crusty texture of the large biscuit, I know that all of my worldly concerns must lift with the first forkful. The flaky pastry pulls apart lingeringly to leave doughy pockets nuzzled by the smooth hotness of gravy. Ah, the gravy.

It is thick and runs silkily on the tongue, with a consistency redolent of fresh pepper and sharpened by salt. Chunks of sausage wallow and roll in this purity, as the gravy spreads over the biscuit and the entire plate. The sausage is of the wet kind, in bulk, though link sausages are common in other versions, but this sausage before me is an immediate delight. Small satchels of the sweet meat are scattered abundantly through the white hotness to give the mixture its delicious flavor. The Bricker's brand of sausage is savored with the usual sage and marjoram, but there is a perfumelike flavor I cannot identify. Perhaps it is nutmeg. Perhaps it is ambrosia.

Since we cannot outlive the gods, we try to out-eat them. Funeral feasts are common to every culture; in every rural community the tables of the bereaved creak beneath covered dishes, pots of stews and platters of cooked meats and fowl. Food seems to be the way we challenge death or the threat of death. If we cannot have the last laugh, we can at least have a last meal. I wonder if the citizens of East Liverpool put on their tuckers for Charles Arthur Floyd, just turned thirty in 1934.

South of East Liverpool, the Ohio River resembles the Rhone River around Valence where that valley narrows as N86 follows the West Bank to give a rolling panorama of an ageless landscape with abrupt hillsides. On Route 7, Kathleen and I can look to our left across the Ohio River to West Virginia. Steep cliffs tower above us, and both landfalls are lushly green in this July light. She has been only mildly curious as to why we are continuing our morning's drive, going on from Brickers toward an unannounced destination rather than return to Pittsburgh. My promise of more birthday celebrations down the road has amused her for she knows of my penchant to keep a festival's lights burning for as long as possible. I have kept secret the pie in Fly, but it is not the only secret I carry down Route 7 on this beautiful day by the Ohio River.

Just a day before our trip, and oddly only a week after I made my will, my doctor tells me that my latest blood test suggests that I have prostate cancer. My PSA count has jumped wildly over the mark, which the medical profession has determined to be the borderline of that forbidding area, but it is a slow-moving disease, he assures me. "Something else will probably get you before it does."

I take the news calmly, possibly because before every visit to his office, I have imagined this scene. His announcement and my response are like a moment we have both rehearsed, and we are letter-perfect. We know our lines. My mind is pulling back for a wider view, and I make some quick calculations based on my score of 4.46. I've had a pretty good time of it; been lucky in love and career and haven't committed too many shameful acts on paper or in person. But, already?

He's been telling me that the next step would be a series of procedures that will probe my prostate gland and then take a biopsy. If those findings are positive, as the blood test has indicated they may be, then some form of radiation therapy will be used. Yes, there may be some unpleasant side effects of the therapy such as impotency, but then, he cheerfully reminds me of the fortuitous rise of Viagra. But he is of a conservative nature and does not rush decisions or treatments, and he wants me to have a second blood test in four months' time before all of the above is done.

So, it his wait-and-see attitude, his reserving a final opinion, that keeps me from telling Kathleen. She sits beside me, happily accompanying the show tunes we have brought on tape in her wonderfully sharp register. Later, she will be angry with me for not telling her and will accuse me of acting like a controlling male, but what was I supposed to say? "Happy Birthday, Darling, the doctor says I have prostate cancer." No, as I savor the two of us making this brilliant passage along the Ohio River, I am thinking that I give the both of us this day, give us Brickers Cafeteria and Deli and with the pie in Fly yet to come. It is a birthday gift for both of us.

Mammoth coal-fed power plants have appeared on both sides of the river. These faceless Goliaths with their slants of chutes angled above them look unattended, seem to process their fuel into electric power without anyone around to monitor the results, as if the men who threw the switches had also transformed themselves into invisible energy, leaving their polished pick-ups behind in the parking lot. At Empire, we pass the dam and locks that control the river's flood stages while permitting a busy passage of tugs and barges, private craft and the ornate reconstructions of large paddlewheelers bringing tourists to Pittsburgh or returning them to St. Louis and New Orleans.

At Steubenville, Route 7 has been renamed Dean Martin Boulevard to commemorate the singer's birthplace and where he came of age in local boxing rings, but on the other side of the city limits, the highway abruptly reverts to Route 7 as if none of that had ever happened. Farther down the road at Martin's Ferry, a modest marker renames the road once again but as the Lou Groza Highway. I tell Kathleen about Lou "The Toe" Groza, the Hall of Fame place-kicker for the Cleveland Browns whose uncanny foot put 1,608 points on the scoreboard. But during that brief biography we have already passed through Martin's Ferry and Route 7 has reclaimed its ordinary identity. At this point in the journey, it would be easy to craft an irony on transient celebrity—these sections of road so vainly renamed—but my fellow Burgher Warhol has already given a time limit to the distance my odometer has routinely registered. West Virginia lies just ahead—Fly is not much farther and the river continues beside us unchanged.

Wheeling is an important manufacturing and commercial hub, and is also a crossroad for U.S. 70, the Intercontinental Highway that runs east and west along the beam of the United States. We are driving south, so we pass under it and at right angles to the overpass of this super-highway, intersecting it but not exactly connecting either. I have made many journeys in many different cars on this road above us, driving west and back to take exits along its route to joy and venture, turning off into self-confidence and renewal—and all those other settlements it had been my good fortune to find along the way.

For as Kathleen sings beside me, I have been going over my accounts, adding up the work and pleasures of this life that has just been given its notice. My mind has turned in a sentimental basting to review my history, to spoon sweet memories over my noble acts. I stir together dollops of my generous behavior with sour portions of betrayal, mixed with the times my inherent virtue has gone unrecognized. It's a tasty dish I set before myself on Route 7.

The dead ask only to be remembered, as Hamlet's father kept asking over and over, but that poor ghost also wanted revenge even if it meant driving his son to madness. And after all, are not last wills sometimes used by the dead to punish the living for just living, documents drafted to get even with survivors for some wounding, some indifference suffered when they all breathed the same atmosphere? Moreover, a will is often a threat compounded beneath the threat of the ultimate threat, but I take pride—following the Ohio River—that the will I have just made has been drawn with love and affection. But other characters have begun to appear at the side of the road, spectral hitchhikers with their hands out and most with the middle finger up. They must be dealt with.

Dante's exile from Florence spurred his masterpiece, a magnificent act of revenge in which he consigned all those who had abused him to terza rimas of hell. Why shouldn't I do the same? Something not so fancy perhaps, but just as satisfying. The editors who have spurned and abandoned me, the feckless agents, the hustlers and gunsels of the writing game, a cowardly critic or two, ambition-crazed careerists, dishonest publishers, a former brother-in-law, one or two old classmates. The list seems endless and we have only reached Powhatan Point! Let me not forget my half-brother who questioned my legitimacy. And the thief who stole my father's cuff links from my cold-water flat in New York, the winter of 1952. Let's see who else? A very large pool of fire for all those that have lied to me or told lies about me, and in a hot tub all to himself will be the man who has abused me so lately. But here's a chance to show charity—to show my good nature—for I will consign this fellow to a moderate temperature, a mediocre flame as befits his character. A slow cooker.

"Slow down," Kathleen warns me. "Why are you driving so fast? You are driving too fast."

And she's right. I am going too fast over this part of Route 7 which has just lost two of its lanes and has become a pleasant and even prettier two-lane highway. We have come nearly seventy miles from East Liverpool, and I look for signs of Fly. The Wayne National forest has just appeared on our right, and its dense stands of black pine soothe me. On the river, a tugboat pushes a string of empty barges north, and the day has become very warm.

One must look closely at Fly, Ohio, because there is not much to see. A filling station, two or three houses, a country saloon and a restaurant called the Riverview. We have driven a hundred miles from East Liverpool, so when I pull into the parking lot of the Riverview, my wife is ready to agree. "It's time for a little pie," I tell her and she nods.

Inside, booths are set around the knotty pine walls and large windows overlook the river and the landing of a small ferry takes travelers back and forth to Sistersville, West Virginia. This service has been operating since 1817 and the current craft is a small paddlewheel that can take up to three cars. Above the middle counter of the restaurant a blackboard lists the day's pies. Every morning at six o'clock, a woman comes in and goes to the kitchen to bake six pies on weekdays and more on Sundays. Here are today's choices: peach, apple, blueberry, coconut custard, lemon meringue, and pumpkin. Another chalked menu announces the plats du jour: baked steak, salmon cakes, rolled cabbage.

My grandmother made salmon cakes on Fridays; canned salmon was cheap during the Depression. The contents of two cans would be mashed together with breadcrumbs, an egg, salt, pepper and chopped celery leaves. The mass divided and shaped into patties that were fried in Crisco and a bit of butter until the edges were crisp. Each patty received a spoonful of white sauce pebbled with fragments of hard-boiled eggs and seasoned with paprika. Sometimes, she would push the whole mixture into one large loaf with thin slices of lemon on top and then bake it to be served with the sauce in an ironstone boat on the side.

"What's that?" my grandfather would always ask, leaning low to peer at the serving platter as if the thing on it was the carcass of a varmint that had become trapped in the rosebushes.

"That's a salmon loaf, Tom," my grandmother would reply wearily.

"A salmon loaf," he would say in wonder. "Well, I'll be damned." And he would pick up the carving knife and fork and do his duty.

Kathleen is saying that the apple pie at the Riverview is very good but does not compare with her mother's. My piece of peach pie has been very satisfying. The crust has been on the short side, crumbly and not too sugared, and the peaches seem fresh. In both pies, there is no suggestion of cornstarch to thicken the filling, but generous portions of fruit fill the space.

What better way to celebrate these treats but to take the ferry across the Ohio River to Sistersville, West Virginia? The craft has been designed to take its lading from either side so as to allow the paddle wheel at the stern room for steerage. We are the only car on this trip. Several wood picnic tables and benches have been set up in one section of the deck, and the wheelhouse stands high above. It's a two-man operation; the guy who has shown us where to park, also closes the gate as the fellow above, his hands resting on the large wheel, looks down on us. Life on the Ohio.

With no ceremony, we have backed off from the riverbank and have turned toward midstream. Kathleen and I embrace in the sun's warmth and kiss as the river's current pulls at the little ferry. Crossing a river has mythical soundings in song and lore, and this particular passage has special meaning for me on this day in July. A school of black bass feeds just ahead, and one breaks surface to leap triumphantly into the air. Looking south, the river flows indolently, a strip of mirror in the light and framed by the midsummer green vegetation along its banks.

We are at midpoint, and this is the place by all the rules of narrative—if only those—that I should tell Kathleen about the test results. The story could almost write itself—the synthesis of place and destiny, the couple departing the one bank to arrive at the other in different circumstances. But I want nothing to change this day, this being with her; nothing to puncture this radiant capsule of time.

As its name suggests, Sistersville was founded by two sisters, the daughters of an early settler. Oil was discovered here in the late nineteenth century to boom the town into a gushing prosperity for a couple of decades with all the banks, trolley lines, and whorehouses a citizen could desire. The village we drive into from the ferry landing today is a sleepy river community with a two-block commercial center where store clerks talk desperately to strangers and a host of antique stores, heavy with patchouli, offer the remnants and cracked vessels of a fabled past. We have turned back toward Pittsburgh, my secret yet shamefully hidden.

By August, my secret still kept, my appetite is sharpened by the appearance of the Marietta tomato in local markets. These fruits from this southern Ohio community are deep red and with a plumpness that beguiles the most casual feel. They are not in the same crate with the dismal produce of Mexico and California. They resemble the tomatoes my grandfather used to grow in our backyard in Kansas City and which gave new meaning to Wonder Bread.

WONDER BREAD TOMATO SANDWICH
(With Marietta tomatoes)
2 slices of fresh Wonder bread—must be sticky fresh.
1 thick slab of Marietta tomato.
1 thin slice of Bermuda onion.
Mayonnaise, salt & pepper.

Slather ample amounts of mayonnaise on both pieces of bread. Place onion, then tomato on one slice. Salt and pepper to taste. Then, place second slice over first and press edges of bread together—all the way around to make a strong seal. Then, bite into this pocket of delight.

Marietta, Ohio, is located 135 miles south of East Liverpool and inland from the river as Route 7 turns west. The tomatoes in the Pittsburgh markets have reminded me also that we stopped at a town restaurant in Marietta several years ago that served a prime example of that classic of all dishes—a hot chicken sandwich with gravy and mashed potatoes. The tang of that gravy over the succulent slices of breast meat on spongy white bread has been kept warm in the back of my memory ever since. I must have that dish again in order to round out the pilgrimage the cicerone in the elevator has set me on.

The rails of old trolley lines yet limn the streets of downtown Marietta, and the pink limestone courthouse holds down one corner of the main intersection. This structure boasts an all-purpose architecture. The first floor is a rough Romanesque that is surmounted by a Palladian temple front and a Sienese bell tower tops both. The people here speak with a pleasant drawl, Kentucky and West Virginia just across the Ohio River, and I feel very much at home. But I cannot remember the name of the restaurant nor where it was located.

Mexican and Asian restaurants seem to be thriving as are several fern bars and coffee spots. One place has a mammoth popcorn maker in its window with a candy counter behind. I peer through other windows, but nothing resembles the pleasant, narrow restaurant that had booths along one wall, a counter and cook area opposite. I can taste that gravy, and my mouth is watering.

At a newsstand, a woman directs me back to the place with the popcorn maker, the First Settler. I had to ask for "The place that serves hot chicken sandwiches." The large machine in the window had obscured the booths in the rear, and I feel vindicated when I enter and my nose prickles with the heavy aroma of chicken gravy. Everything now is as I remember it. I take one of the booths. Two men at the counter drink coffee and talk loudly of backhoes. Several booths down, a very old lady carefully spoons soup into her mouth, looking blankly around after each swallow as if trying to determine the flavor.

We are the only customers in the booths served by a pleasant young woman wearing a ruffled apron over slacks and sweater. Two women work behind the counter; one at the stove and steam table and the other to serve and this person has just refilled the coffee cups of the two men. One has just said something to her that makes her laugh a little—after she thinks about it.

Meanwhile, the waitress has brought me a menu and a glass of water. I don't open the menu; I know what I want. "I'll have that hot chicken sandwich with mashed potatoes and gravy," I tell her. She looks troubled.

"We have deep fried chicken. We don't have a hot chicken sandwich," she says.

"You used to have it."

Her eyes shift nervously. "Mary Anne," she cries, and the woman at the griddle looks our way. She checks the items cooking and walks toward us, a worried look on her face. I could be a traveler making an untoward advance on her younger colleague, an oaf without the savoir faire of the local at the counter.

Circumspectly, I describe the dish I ate in this very spot, perhaps this very same booth, just a few years back. She looks dubious. I want to get up and leave. But maybe this disappointment is meant to prepare me for all the last meals to come; that I must eat whatever they might be. We must accept what can be put together at the last moment, thrown together from whatever is on hand. In fact, the older woman is offering me an improvisation.

"I can take some of that deep fried and lie it on some bread and put gravy over."

"And mashed potatoes?"

She smiles. "Sure mashed potatoes too."

When the young waitress returns with this spontaneous creation, she is beaming, and I feel a little like Robinson Crusoe, making a new life out of a salvaged past. Moreover, in this one desperate stroke, I have probably enlarged the menu of the New Settler, and that is something of a legacy. She has paused after putting the plate before me, as if to join me in the appreciation of what we have created. Then she leaves me to my pleasure.

The gravy that spills over the sandwich and settles into the cone of mashed potatoes is a chicken-leg yellow and with an intense flavor on the salty side. The slices of chicken beneath are crunchy on the edges and not the tender slices of meat I have craved. The white bread is acceptable and the mashed potatoes smoothly made. It's a filling meal. I've been given a small salad, and several chunks of tomato, lying in shavings of iceberg lettuce, quickly interest me. They are tasteless pulps. Where is the Marietta tomato?

"We import the tomatoes," the cook tells me as I pay the bill. In fact she seems unaware of the magnificent fruit that grows somewhere in her town, perhaps within walking distance of The New Settler. The young waitress could easily walk out to the farm and bring back an apron full by lunchtime. "My dad raises tomatoes," the woman muses as she hands me my change. "They just keep coming on, and I guess we could bring some of them to the restaurant."

Driving back to Pittsburgh, no longer hungry but still with an appetite, I look forward to dinner with Kathleen. One good meal will make up for a poor one; it is the hope that keeps us going from table to table, seeking the perfect meal—or even the perfect tomato. Kathleen waits for me in Pittsburgh, and later, the results of my second PSA test will indicate my score has dropped down into the safe area. No further probing is necessary, my doctor will say. It is only a reprieve, of course, and my journey continues north on Route 7 back through Fly and then East Liverpool. Damn death and damn all that threaten death. I look forward to the next meal. And the next. And the next.

Acknowledgments

Some of these essays have appeared in different versions in these publications, which have my thanks for originally publishing them and for their permission to use them in this collection.

"Going to Cuba," *Sewanee Review;* "Making It Up," "Winfield Townley Scott," "So Long, Natty Bumppo," and "In Montaigne's Tower," *Ohio Review;* "Disorderly Conduct," *New England Review;* "About Hilary," *Washington Post;* "Passing through Pittsburgh," *Creative Non-Fiction;* "My Father's Image" and "Leaving the Party," *New Letters;* "Everyone Was Alive in 1924," *Heart Quarterly;* "Connections," *Virginia Quarterly Review;* "Son of Spoon River," *The Essayist at Work.*

The author is also grateful to the editors who singled out three of these essays for particular notice: the Monroe Spears Award of the *Sewanee Review* to "Going to Cuba"; the Anchor Best Essays of 1998, edited by Phillip Lopate, to "In Montaigne's Tower"; and Best Essays American Essays of 1999, chosen by Edward Hoagland and Robert Atwan, to "Making It Up."

Also thanks to Carnegie Mellon.

About the Author

Photo by Kathleen George

Hilary Masters's eight novels include *Clemmons, Cooper, Strickland,* and *Home Is the Exile.* His short fiction has been singled out by both the *Pushcart Prize* and *Best American Short Stories* and has also received the Emily Balch Award from the *Virginia Quarterly Review.* He lives in Pittsburgh, Pennsylvania.